そのまま使える

Ready-to-use
Architectural
English Expressions
by Yama / Kazuya Yamazaki

建築英語表現

山嵜一也 著

学芸出版社

はじめに

英語の電話が取れますか？

　2001年に私は単身渡英したのですが、実務経験も英語力もほとんどありませんでした。何とか就職先の設計事務所を見つけたものの、すぐに電話恐怖症に陥っていました。デスクの電話を取り上げれば、当たり前ですがネイティブの相手は容赦ない英語でまくしたててきます。私はしどろもどろになり、なんとかやり過ごし、受話器を置くと落ち込みました。それを繰り返しているうち電話恐怖症になり、電話が鳴ると急に書類を探すふりをしたり、トイレに立ち上がったりしてごまかしていました。しかし、一人留守番をして、いよいよ受話器を取らざるを得ない状況では背中に冷たい汗を感じながら対応したものです。

　こうやって始まった私の海外実務経験は12年間にわたりました。渡英前の英語力は所詮日本の英語教育によるものでしかありません。ですから本書に紹介される英語は建築の実務を通して培ったものと言えます。

　本書を手に取った方は、既に日本から海外プロジェクトに携わることで現地の設計事務所と協働して仕事を進めているかもしれません。また、留学や海外就職という野望を胸に秘めているのかも。あるいは最近ではネットを通じた海外メディアへの情報発信に向けてプレスリリース作成に迫られているのでしょうか。いずれにせよ、言語は具体的な必要に迫られてこそ身に着きます。

　このような本を出版していて逆説的ですが、英語を身に着けるには仕事の現場で嫌な思い、悔しい思い、そして冷や汗をかく経験を積み重ねることが

大切だと思います。それでは、現場で英語を活用する機会がなければ永遠に身に着かないのでしょうか。私自身を振り返ってみれば、やはりその時に備えておくに越したことはない、と感じます。

英語のコミュニケーションスキルである「聞く」「話す」「読む」「書く」の4つのうち、独学が可能なのはインプット系の「聞く」「読む」でしょう。まずこの2つのスキルをある程度身に着ければ、アウトプット系の「話す」「書く」に対しても多少余裕を持って対応で

勤務先デスクの風景。電話が鳴るのが本当に恐怖でした。

きる。電話の受け答えだって、少なくとも当時の私よりは自信をもって臨めるはずです。

本書では建築の実務現場、設計からプレゼンテーション、施工の現場までプロセスに沿った85の場面を想定し、私自身の経験をもとにできる限り具体的な会話例を集めました。

読者の皆様が世界の建築現場で活躍するときに寄り添うお守りのような本を目指しました。

2016年8月　山嵜一也

STEP.1 デザインの魅力を伝える ...9
Conveying Design Ideas

1	敷地・配置　Site/Location	10
2	周辺環境①（自然環境）　Natural Environment	12
3	周辺環境②（街並み）　Townscape	14
4	外構　External Work	16
5	庭　Garden	18
6	植栽　Planting	20
7	広場・公園　Square/Park	22
8	アプローチ・エントランス　Approach/Entrance	24
9	ボリューム　Volume	26
10	ファサード　Facade	28
11	形状　Form	30
12	状態　Situation/Condition (of the site)	32
13	個人住宅　Private House	34
14	集合住宅　Housing Complex	36
15	オフィス　Office	38
16	公共建築　Public Building	40
17	公共空間　Public Space	42
18	商業施設①（小規模〜中規模店舗）　Commercial Building (small to medium scale)	44
19	商業施設②（複合商業施設）　Commercial Building (complex type)	46
20	建築テーマ①（ローコスト）　Low-cost Architecture	48
21	建築テーマ②（エコ・サステイナブル）　Ecological/Sustainable Architecture	50
22	建築テーマ③（リノベーション）　Renovation/Refurbishment	52
23	部屋の機能　Function	54
24	平面計画　Planning	56
25	動線・シークエンス　Circulation/Sequence	58
26	眺望　View	60
27	開口部　Opening	62

28	窓　Window	64
29	空間表現①（スケール・サイズ）　Scale/Size	66
30	空間表現②（閉じる・開く）　Close/Open	68
31	空間表現③（曖昧な表現）　Ambiguous Expression	70
32	空間表現④（程度）　Grade	72
33	色（濃淡・明度・彩度）　Color/Shading/Brightness/Chroma	74
34	テクスチャー　Texture	76
35	明るさ・照明　Brightness/Lighting	78
36	透明度　Transparency	80
37	インテリア①（各地のスタイル）　Interior（local styles）	82
38	インテリア②（本物・偽物）　Interior（Authentic/Fake）	84
39	家具とその配置　Furniture and Layout	86
40	仕上げ①（外装）　Cladding Exterior	88
41	仕上げ②（内装）　Interior	90
42	アクティビティ　Activity	92
43	日本特有の法規　Japanese Construction Law	94
44	法規　Construction Law	96
45	構造　Structure	98
46	構法　Construction Method	100
47	設備　Services	102
48	防火・耐火　Fire Protection/Fire Resistance	104
49	断熱・換気　Heat/Insulation/Ventilation	106
50	防犯・セキュリティ　Security	108
51	建築環境　Architectural Environment	110

コラム①
英語に直訳する前に、まず日本語をシンプルに　　　　　　　　　　　　112

STEP.2 プレゼンテーション・テクニック
Presentation Techniques

... 113

52	プレゼンテーションを始める　Starting a Presentation	114
53	提案する　Proposing Ideas	116
54	根拠・理由・例を示す　Giving Reasons and Examples	118
55	強調する・比べる・言い換える　Emphasizing/Comparing/Paraphrasing	120
56	将来の話をする　Talking about the Future	122
57	実現可能性　Feasibility	124
58	コストの説明をする　Explaining the Cost	126
59	メンテナンスへの配慮を説明する　Explaining Maintenance Arrangements	128
60	オプションを提示する　Proposing Options	130
61	メリット・デメリットを説明する　Explaining the Advantages and Disadvantages	132
62	質問をする　Asking Questions	134
63	即答を避ける　Avoiding a Quick Response	136
64	締めくくる　Concluing Business	138
65	コンペティションへの応募　Entry to a Competition	140
66	提案書の作成　Creaing a Proposal Document	142
67	プレゼン用データの作成　Creating Presentation Data	144
68	プレスリリースで使う表現　Expressions for Press Release	146

コラム②
プレゼン。相手の目線で考える。　　　　　　　　　　　　　　148

STEP.3 現場のコミュニケーション
Communication in Practice ...149

69	資料の確認・受け渡し	Confirming the Document and Handing it Over	150
70	お願いの仕方	How to Make a Request	152
71	請求・支払い	Billing/Payment	154
72	契約	Contract	156
73	役割分担の確認	Confirmation of Roles	158
74	スケジュールの確認	Confirmation of Schedule	160
75	進行管理	Schedule Management	162
76	コスト管理	Cost Management	164
77	現地調査	Site Survey	166
78	基本設計	Preliminary Design	168
79	見積もり	Estimation/Quotation	170
80	実施設計	Construction Design	172
81	施工現場	Construction Site	174
82	納まりの施工	Construction Details	176
83	納まりの表現	Expressions about Details	178
84	竣工・引き渡し	Completion/Delivery	180
85	撮影・画像処理	Photo Shoot/Image Processing	182

コラム③
会議には70%の気持ちで臨む（事前準備は120%で）　184

英語索引　188
日本語索引　198

この本の使い方

examples
現場での典型的な場面を想定した会話例です。まずは身近な場面、必要な場面から選んで使っても良いでしょう。

key phrases
例文の中でも特に便利なフレーズを選び出し、類似表現も加えました。そのまま覚えて活用してください。

---

01 敷地・配置
Site/Location

提案するアイデアが如何に対象敷地に適しているかをプレゼンテーションしていきます。その際、現場の周辺環境はさることながら日本とは違う現地の気候風土などに正面から向き合わなければなりません。それを的確に図面およびプレゼンテーション資料に盛り込んで行きます。

examples

- The external walls were set 3m back from the site boundary.
  外壁を敷地境界線から3m内側にしました。
- The parameter lines on the drawings were drawn with a dot-dash line.
  図面上の敷地境界線は一点鎖線で描きました。
- The spacious courtyard is located in the center of the building.
  大きな中庭を建物中央部に配置しました。
- The reflection of the adjacent house appears in the window because of the site in a dense area.
  敷地が密集地にあるため、窓に隣の建物が映り込んでいます。
- The site connects to the front road via a long promenade.
  敷地は長いプロムナードで前面道路に接道してます。
- The long narrow building is designed to fit in the long rectangular shape of the site.
  長い長方形の敷地形状に納まるように細長い建築を計画しました。

key phrases

set back~from
〜から後退した
The building should be set 2m back from the street.
その建物は道路から2m後退しなければならない。

locate~in the center of…
〜を…の中心に据える

because of
〜という理由から。続くのは名詞。
似た意味で due to 〜のために。to の後には名詞が続く。
Due to a late decision, the whole process was pushed back.
遅い決定により、すべての過程が後退した。

connect to the front road
前面道路に接する

fit in
〜に納まる。他に fit within 〜の中に納まる。
The chest fits into the wall recess.
収納タンスが壁の奥まった場所に納まりました。

vocabulary

- external 外の
- site boundary, parameter lines 敷地境界線
- dot-dash line 一点鎖線
- spacious (空間的に) 広い
- courtyard 中庭
- locate 〜に据える
- adjacent house 隣家
- reflection 反射
- dense area 密集地
- front road 前面道路
- via 〜を介して
- promenade 遊歩道
- rectangular 長方形 (四角形) の

Quick Chat 咄嗟のひとこと
Q: Why is the parking area behind the building?
なぜ、駐車場が建物の裏にあるのですか?
A: In order to keep safe customers.
利用者の安全性を確保するためです。

Quick Chat 咄嗟のひとこと
突然投げかけられる問いや指摘への答え方の例です。電話や会議などでのやりとりを想定してみてください。

vocabulary
examples や key phrases で使われた語彙を中心にまとめています。特に頻繁に使われる部位や仕上げなどに関する図解もしました。

Ready-to-use
Architectural
English
Expressions

STEP.1

デザインの魅力を伝える

Conveying Design Ideas

敷地・配置
01 Site/Location

アイデアを提案する際、いかに対象敷地に適しているかをプレゼンテーションしていきます。それを的確に図面およびプレゼンテーション資料に盛り込む英語表現が求められます。

examples

- The external walls were set 3m back from the site boundary.
  外壁は敷地境界線から 3m 内側にしました。

- The parameter lines on the drawings were drawn with a dot-dash line.
  図面上の敷地境界線は一点鎖線で描きました。

- The spacious courtyard is located in the center of the building.
  大きな中庭を建物中央部に配置しています。

- The reflection of the adjacent house appears in the window because the site is in a dense area.
  敷地が密集地にあるため、窓に隣の建物が映り込んでしまいます。

- The site connects to the front road via a long promenade.
  敷地は長いプロムナードで前面道路に接道してます。

- The long narrow building is designed to fit in the long rectangular shape of the site.
  長い長方形の敷地形状に納まるように細長い建築を計画しています。

Quick Chat | 咄嗟のひとこと

- Why is the parking area behind the building?
  なぜ、駐車場が建物の裏にあるのですか？

key phrases

set back from~
～から後退した
The building should be set 2m back from the street.
その建物は道路から 2m 後退しなければならない。

locate A in the center of B
A を B の中心に据える

because~
～という理由から。名詞が続く類似表現に because of~ や due to~ がある。
Due to a late decision, the whole process was pushed back.
遅い決定により、すべての過程が後退した。

connect to the front road
前面道路に接する

fit in~
～に納まる。他に fit within~/ ～の中に納まる。
The chest fits in the wall recess.
収納タンスが壁の奥まった場所に納まりました。

---

vocabulary

external　外の	adjacent house　隣家
site boundary, parameter lines　敷地境界線	reflection　反射
dot-dash line　一点鎖線	dense area　密集地
spacious　(空間的に) 広い	front road　前面道路
courtyard　中庭	via　介して
locate　据える	promenade　遊歩道
	rectangular　長方形 (四角形) の

 In order to keep customers safe.
利用者の安全性を確保するためです。

02 周辺環境① （自然環境）
Natural Environment

現場の周辺環境はさることながら日本とは違う現地の気候風土などに正面から向き合わなければなりません。周辺環境をきちんと資料や図面に表現し、説明することで、主役である建物をより際立たせることができます。

examples

- The project will start with an exploration of the natural environment around the site.
  計画は敷地周囲の自然環境を読み解くところから始まる。

- The building should be harmonized with the environment around the site.
  建築は敷地周辺環境との調和を図らなければならない。

- The site is on a sloping ground facing the coast.
  敷地は傾斜地にあり海に面しています。

- Sites surrounded by rice fields are a typical scene in farming villages in Japan.
  周囲が田んぼに囲まれた敷地は典型的な日本の農村風景です。

- Sites surrounded by mountains at the rear are prosperous areas for the fishing industry.
  背後を山に囲まれた敷地は漁業の盛んな土地です。

- The layout of every room has been designed to give views of the wild nature around the site.
  すべての部屋から建物周辺の野生の自然を眺められるような配置計画としました。

Quick Chat ｜ 咄嗟のひとこと

- Is this site near the main road?
  敷地が幹線道路沿いですよね。

key phrases

start with~
～から始める。作業や行為を始める際に使用。似た表現に begin with～ などもある。

harmonize with~
～と調和する。建築の周辺環境との調和に使用。harmonize A with B/A と B を調和させる。

be surrounded by~
～で周辺を囲まれている。建物の周辺環境を説明するときに使える。
surrounded by the high wall 周辺を高い壁で囲われている。

typical scene
典型的な風景。他に scenery around 周囲の景色。scenery along the valley 渓谷沿いの風景。have a view of～/ ～の景色を得る、～が見える、～を望む。

at the rear
背後で、背後を

design to give views of~
～を眺められるよう計画する

that's why~
それゆえに～

vocabulary

explore 読み解く	prosperous 栄えた、盛んな
environment 環境	fishing industry 漁業
sloping ground 傾斜地	wild nature 野生の自然
coast 海岸	main road 幹線道路
farming village 農村	solution 解法

 Yes, that's why we have proposed the solution of a closed building.
はい、それゆえに私たちは閉じた建築という解法を提案しました。

周辺環境② (街並み)
Townscape

日本の街並みは世界から見ても特殊な環境に映ります。それゆえ、写真やスケッチを活用するだけでなく、言葉でも詳細に説明することで、プレゼンを受け取る側もイメージを喚起しやすくなるはずです。

examples

- Electricity poles that are a unique aspect of Japanese cities appear right in front of buildings.
  日本特有の電柱が建物のすぐ前に現れることになります。

- It is hard to take photos of the whole facade due to the narrowness of the street in front of the site.
  敷地前の道路が狭いのでファサード全体を撮影するのは難しい。

- We considered the residents' privacy due to the dense area.
  密集地なので、住人のプライバシーに配慮しました。

- The courtyard is set within the building to escape the bustle of the city.
  都会の喧騒から逃れるため建物内に中庭を設けます。

- After a series of redevelopments, the industrial area has been transformed into a shopping area.
  一連の再開発の後、工業地域が商業地域に生まれ変わりました。

Quick Chat | 咄嗟のひとこと

What are the surrounding buildings like?
周辺の建物はどんな感じですか？

key phrases

in front of~
～の前に。類似表現に right in front of~/ ～のすぐ前に、と強調になる。
The bus stop is located right in front of the station.
バス停は駅のすぐ前に配置しました。

it is hard to~
～することは困難だ

consider privacy
プライバシーに配慮する

transform into~
～へ変身する。～へ生まれ変わる。形態の変形だけでなく、街並みの変化などの表現にも使う。

be not unified
統一感がない

vocabulary

electricity pole	電柱	bustle	喧騒
facade	立面、ファサード	redevelopment	再開発
narrowness	狭さ、細さ	surrounding buildings	周辺の建物

 The area in front of the station is not unified.
駅前周辺は統一感がありません。

04 外構
External Work

都心部の建物が密集した地域や郊外の空の広がる地域など、外構計画を説明するにはその周辺情報も同時に伝える必要があります。

examples

- ► The drainage covered with gravel is located under the roof eaves.
  砂利に覆われた排水溝は屋根の庇の下にあります。

- ► The wall is erected around the site to block the view from the adjacent building.
  隣の建物からの視線を遮るため塀が敷地周囲に設けられています。

- ► The number of disabled parking space is calculated based on the number of visitors.
  利用者数に合わせて車いす専用駐車場の数も算出されています。

- ► The key lock system has been installed at the bike parking area for security.
  防犯のため、駐輪場に施錠装置を設置しました。

- ► The height of the hedge shuts out the view from outside while still providing a sense of the atmosphere from outside.
  生垣の高さは外からの視線は遮りつつ、一方で外の様子を感じられる高さです。

- ► Mirror-polished granite stone has been installed at the entrance.
  鏡面仕上げの御影石が玄関に使用されました。

Quick Chat | 咄嗟のひとこと

- ❓ What material is used for the hedge?
  生垣は何で出来ていますか？

key phrases

cover with~
〜で覆う。建築の植栽などが覆うという場面は多数あるので、多用するイディオム。

locate under~
〜の下に位置する。locate above〜/ 〜の上に位置する。
The roof eaves are located above the drainage.
屋根の庇は排水溝の上に位置しています。

block the view
景色を遮る。block には塊と言う意味もあるが、遮る、という動詞もある。shut out the view も同義。

disabled parking space
障がい者専用駐車場。日本でいうところの車いす専用駐車場の意味。

based on~
〜を元に、〜を基準に。数値などを勘案するときの基準や法則を説明する際に使用。
The building form is designed based on the orientation of the site.
建物の形は敷地の方位に基づいてデザインされている。

for security
防犯のために
A kiosk should be locked at night for security.
キオスクは夜間の防犯のために施錠するべきです。

while~
〜の一方で

provide a sense of
〜する感じを与える

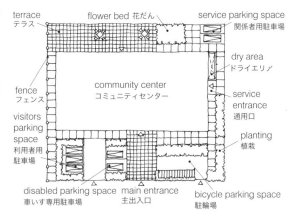

公共施設の外構例

vocabulary

drainage 排水溝	disabled parking space 車いす専用駐車場
gravel 砂利	install 設置する
roof eaves 屋根庇、軒	hedge 生垣
erect 建てる	mirror polished 鏡面仕上げの
adjacent 隣接した	granite stone 御影石

 Bamboo. It's a cheap but tough material.
竹です。安価ですが丈夫です。

庭
Garden

世界から見た日本の庭、庭園は禅の思想が投影され、神秘的、魅力的に映ります。日本人建築士に仕事を依頼する以上、海外のクライアントはあなたがその背景を得ているものとして話をしてきます。日本の庭に関する基本的な知識とともに英語表現も備えておきましょう。

examples

- A dry landscape garden was adopted in order to show the imaginary water flow.
  想像上の水の流れを演出するために枯山水庭園を採用しました。

- A series of stones makes use of the landscape visible in the background, a concept known in Japan as *shakkei*.
  一連の石の配置は敷地背後の山の眺めを日本で言うところの借景として利用します。

- With the same finish floor level, the living room is like a part of the garden terrace.
  床面の仕上げ高さを同じにすることで居間は庭のようになります。

- Let's think about whether to install a rooftop garden or solar panels.
  屋上庭園とするか、太陽光発電を設置するか、考えてみましょう。

- For a commercial building, even a tiny garden can be a luxurious presentation.
  商業施設にとって、たとえ小さな庭でも贅沢な演出になるはずです。

- The scarcement area around the building is paved with black gravel.
  建物周囲の犬走り部には黒砂利を敷き詰めます。

🎙 Quick Chat | 咄嗟のひとこと

 Isn't this garden too small?
この庭は小さすぎないか？

key phrases

dry landscape garden
枯山水庭園。枯れた庭→枯山水庭園という意味。海外では日本の枯山水は鑑賞庭として好まれる。

a series of~
一連の〜。個別ではなく一つのグループとして表現するイディオム。
A series of light fittings are allocated along the same line.
一連の照明は同線上に位置している。

make use of the landscape (of)~
〜を借景として利用する

with the same finish floor level
同じ仕上げ面高さで。finish floor level は略語で FFL。図面上では▽FFL など表現される。

a part of~
〜の一部として。全体の一部分に注目して表現する。
His reading space is planned in a part of the living space.
彼の書斎スペースは居間の一部に計画されている。

whether to install A or B
A を設置するか、B を設置するか

be paved with~
〜で舗装される。pavement 歩道。

---

vocabulary

imaginary water flow　想像上の水の流れ
finish　仕上げ
rooftop garden　屋上庭園
solar panel　太陽光発電
commercial building　商業施設
luxurious presentation　贅沢な演出
scarcement　犬走り
gravel　砂利
spot garden　坪庭

 In Japan, we have the idea of *tsuboniwa*, or spot gardens.
日本には坪庭という考えがあります。

06 植栽
Planting

植栽には計画地のある地域に相応しい樹木を使うことが多いので、英語の名称だけでなくその特徴を調べた上で説明を加える必要があります。また、日本を感じさせる、すなわち「和」を感じさせる植栽とはどのようなものがあるのか、またその英語表現にどのようなものがあるのかをリサーチしておく必要もあります。

examples

- The planting plan involves the generous use of cherry trees to convey a sense of beautiful spring.
  植栽計画は春の訪れを感じられる桜の木をふんだんに配置します。

- An evergreen tree is used in the courtyard for easy maintenance.
  簡単なメンテナンスのために、中庭には常緑樹を採用しています。

- An insect-proof plant was selected for the wall.
  虫害に強い植栽を壁面に選定しました。

- A bamboo forest was utilized at the entrance to create an Asian atmosphere.
  竹林を玄関道に活用することでアジア風を表現しました。

- We would love to use local plants.
  地元の樹木を積極的に取り入れたい。

- We are looking for plants with delicate leaves, e.g. flower petals.
  花びらのような繊細な葉の木を探しています。

Quick Chat | 咄嗟のひとこと

What kind of planting would suit here?
ここにはどんな植栽が合うでしょうか。

key phrases

generous use of~
〜を気前よく使うこと。類似表現に full of~/〜でいっぱいの、〜で満ちた、〜でたくさんの。ふんだんにある状態を表す意味。
At weekends, the park is full of families.
週末の公園はたくさんの家族でにぎわう。

convey a sense of~
〜の感じを出す。sense of~/〜に対する感覚。sense of color 色彩感覚。sense of material 素材に対する感覚。

for maintenance
メンテナンスに配慮して。丁寧な表現になると for maintenance reasons でメンテナンスの理由から。

insect-proof
防虫。proof には防止という意味。メンテナンスのことを考えた時に、〜に強い、〜に耐性があるというのは説得材料になる。派生語として waterproof（防水）、earthquake-proof（耐震）、shock-proof（防振）など。

create atmosphere
雰囲気を生む

would love to~
ぜひ〜したい。丁寧に要望を伝える would like to~（〜をしたい）より強い表現。

e.g.~
〜のような。for example に置き換えられる。類似表現に such as~ がある。
Different types of materials are used on the external floor, such as a metal checker plate.
例えば、鉄製のチェッカープレートなど、異なる種類の建材が外構床に使われています。

---

vocabulary

planting plan 植栽計画	bamboo forest 竹林
cherry tree 桜	Asian atmosphere アジア風
evergreen tree 常緑樹	flower petal 花弁
maintenance 維持管理	filtered sunlight 木漏れ日
insect 虫	

 It would be fantastic if we could have a wooded area with filtered sunlight.
木漏れ日のある雑木林があると素敵だと思います。

広場・公園
Square/Park

日本の都心部に見られる「広場」は公開空地やアトリウムのような内部空間にもあるため、欧米の「広場」や「公園」とは違った意味合いを持ちます。日本特有の広場・公園の成り立ちを説明できると相手に伝わります。

examples

- Strong winds in the public spaces near tall buildings should be taken into consideration.
  高層ビルに隣接する広場は強い風に配慮しなければならない。

- This square is a public open space created as part of a comprehensive design system in accordance with the architectural standards law in Japan.
  この広場は日本の建築基準法に基づく総合設計制度により設けられた公開空地です。

- The impression given by the pocket park is totally changed with the use of grass and water.
  小さな公園の印象は芝生と水を使うことで大きく変わります。

- Special consideration of the air conditioning will be required if the atrium is to become a public space.
  アトリウムが公共空間となるためには空調に特別な配慮が必要となるでしょう。

- The intersection of passageways can be turned into a square simply by installing benches.
  路地の交差点はベンチを置くだけで広場になります。

Quick Chat | 咄嗟のひとこと

Q: How should we use the surrounding unused space?
余裕のある周辺スペースはどう活用しようか？

key phrases

take into consideration
配慮する

public open space created as part of a comprehensive design system
総合設計制度により設けられた公開空地

in accordance with~
〜に基づいて、〜に従って。関連表現に according to~/ 〜によると。
According to the sign, we can't smoke in this area.
案内表示によるとこの場所で喫煙できません。

architectural standards law
建築基準法。building standards law とも言う。

intersection
交差する場所。交差点。道路の交差点には他に traffic crossing、junction などがある。
intersect〔動詞〕。intersecting walls 交差している壁。

turn into ~
〜になる

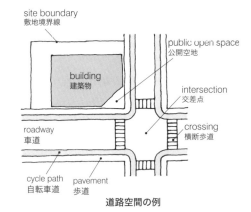

道路空間の例

vocabulary

strong wind 強風	air conditioning 空調
square 広場	atrium アトリウム、吹き抜け
public open space 公開空地	passageway 遊歩道
comprehensive 総合的な	install 設置する
totally 全体的に	bench ベンチ

 Why don't we introduce a rental cycle docking station?
レンタルサイクルのステーションなんてどうでしょうか？

アプローチ・エントランス
Approach/Entrance

建物へのアプローチは方位、距離、使われ方などの表現が多用されます。またエントランスまでの奥行きの表現や、都心部の密集地では一目でエントランスとわかる表現が求められます。

examples

- High-grade materials were used for surfaces in the main entrance.
  主玄関にはグレードの高い建材を選びました。

- The visitors approach the building via the gravel path.
  訪問者は玉砂利を敷いた道から建物に入ってきます。

- The approach to the stadium has the effect of lifting the spirits of spectators before the event.
  競技場へのアプローチは観客にイベント前の気分を高める効果がある。

- The entrance of the station should have a slip-resistant floor.
  駅のエントランスは滑り防止床とするべきです。

- An auto-locking system prevents people from outside entering the communal space of the building.
  オートロックシステムが外部から人が建物の共用部へ入るのを防ぎます。

- A freestanding wall has been installed in the entrance hall of the restaurant.
  レストランのエントランスには受け壁を設けた。

Quick Chat │ 咄嗟のひとこと

Does the entrance face north?
エントランスが北向きなのですか？

key phrases

approach A via B
B を経て A につながる、B を経由して A に近づく
The auditorium is approached via this promenade.
この遊歩道は音楽堂へつながっています。

have the effect of~
～の効果がある、～の機能がある
The corridor has the additional effect of promoting communication.
この廊下はコミュニケーションを取るというもう一つの機能があります。

lift the spirits
気分を高める、高揚させる

slip-resistant
滑り止めの。resistance〔名詞〕は防止、耐性。前出の proof のように water resistant, shock resistant など。利用者の安全性を確保する際に用いる表現。

prevent A from B
A が B を防ぐ

communal space
共用空間。集合住宅などの中庭は communal garden などと呼ぶ。

maintain privacy
プライバシーを保つ

---

vocabulary

high-grade material　高品質建材	effect　効果
main entrance　主玄関	spectators　観客
approach　続く	auto-locking system　オートロック
via　通過して	freestanding wall　受け壁
gravel path　砂利の小路	maintain　保つ、守る
stadium　競技場	

 Yes, in order to maintain tenants' privacy.
はい、居住者のプライバシーを保つためです。

ボリューム
Volume

日本の建築空間は伝統的にボリュームの境界を曖昧にすることが多くあります。その曖昧さに込められている意味をうまく表現できれば、欧米の建築と差別化された提案となり得ます。

examples

▶ The entrance hall has a two-storey height volume in order to welcome the guests.
玄関は来客を歓迎するため二層吹き抜けボリュームとします。

▶ The insertion of external spaces into the house on this tiny site turns it into a microcosmos.
この小さな敷地の住宅は屋外空間を挿入することで小宇宙を生み出します。

▶ The spaces between the randomly laid small blocks become ambiguous places that are neither interior nor exterior.
ランダムに配置された小さなブロックの間の空間は屋内でも屋外でもない曖昧な場所となります。

▶ We have a concept of *engawa*, which is the buffer zone between external and internal space.
私たちには外部と内部の緩衝帯となる縁側という考え方あります。

▶ Urban residences in tight locations can gain spaciousness with high ceilings.
わずかな敷地の都市型住宅は天井を高くすることで開放感を得ます。

▶ The building doesn't feel oppressive even though the maximum floor-area ratio has been used on the site.
敷地容積率いっぱいに使ったわりには建物に圧迫感はありません。

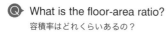

Quick Chat ｜咄嗟のひとこと

Q What is the floor-area ratio?
容積率はどれくらいあるの？

key phrases

two-storey height volume
二層分の高さのあるボリューム。層、階は storey。three-storey house 三階建て住宅。

randomly laid
ランダムに配置された。規則性、恣意性のないデザインの時に使用する表現。laid は lay（横たえる、置く）の過去・過去分詞形。

become an ambiguous place
曖昧な場所となる

neither interior nor exterior
内部でも外部でもない。neiher A nor B/A でもなく、B でもない。どちらにも属さない、曖昧な状態を説明する際に使用する表現。逆に、内部でもあり外部でもあるは both interior and exterior.

a concept of~
〜という考え。an idea of~ なども同様。

feel oppressive
圧迫感がある

Those buildings on the street feel oppressive.
その通りに建つ建物には圧迫感がある。

use the maximum floor area ratio
容積率を最大限に使う

---

vocabulary

welcome　歓迎する	external　外部の
insert　挿入する	internal　内部の
tiny site　小さな敷地	tight location　わずかな敷地
microcosmos　小宇宙	gain　得る
randomly　ランダムに、不規則に	spaciousness　広大さ、開放感
ambiguous　曖昧な	floor-area ratio　容積率
buffer zone　緩衝帯	

Ⓐ It is two hundred percent.
200 パーセントです。

10 ファサード
Facade

海外の国と地域によって異なる景観への配慮が求められます。一方で欧米諸国に比べて景観規制の弱い日本ではその突拍子もないファサードデザインが注目を集める要素になり得ます。

examples

- ▶ The facade is divided into several different sizes and uses various materials to avoid any feeling of oppressiveness.
  圧迫感が出ないように、ファサードは様々な大きさに分割し色々な素材を使用しています。

- ▶ The grooved grid lines on elevations make its expression softer.
  格子状の溝が立面の表情を柔らかくします。

- ▶ The height of the windows was aligned with that of the adjacent building.
  窓の高さは隣地の建物の窓の高さに合わせた。

- ▶ The corners of the buildings are chamfered in order to create a natural flow on the town corners.
  建物の角を面取りして、角地に動線の流れを作っています。

- ▶ The building opens onto the external area.
  建物は外部に開けています。

- ▶ The front facade expresses luxury design whilst the rear has a lived-in feel.
  表のファサードは高級感を、裏のファサードは生活感を出しています。

- ▶ We designed a facade suitable for a commercial building.
  商業施設に相応しいファサードをデザインしました。

💡 Quick Chat | 咄嗟のひとこと

- ❓ The neighbors are concerned about the reflection from the facade.
  近隣からファサードの反射の懸念が出ています。

key phrases

divide into~
～に分ける。関連語に divider 仕切り。
The main facade is divided into three by joints.
メインファサードは目地により3つに分割されています。

avoid a feeling of oppressiveness
圧迫感を避ける。圧迫感には pressure もある。
The top of the wall is tilted to avoid pressure.
壁上部は圧迫感を避けるために傾いています。

align with~
～に合わせる。施工図面で面が合っているなど施工者への注意喚起でも用いられる。
The bottom of the panel aligns with the top of the counter.
パネルの下部の位置はカウンタートップと合わせてください。

chamfer
角を削る。面取りする。建築部材の仕上げ方法としても覚えておきたい用語。
chamfered corner 面取りされた角。

create a flow
流れを作る。ものの流れ、ものの動きが出来るときに使う。
The gutter angle is insufficient to make rain water flow.
溝の傾斜角度が雨水が流れるのに十分ではない。

whilst~
一方で。while と同様に使う。
This product is high in quality, while also having an affordable price.
この製品はお手頃の価格でありながら、良い品質です。

---

vocabulary

several	様々な	lived-in feel	生活感
material	素材、建材	suitable	相応しい
groove	溝	tilted	傾いた
grid line	グリッド線、格子状の線	gutter	溝
elevation	立面	insufficient	不十分な
corner	角	high in quality	高品質な
chamfer	面取りする	affordable price	手頃な価格

Ⓐ But the percentage of glass reflection is below the standard reflectance value.　しかし、ガラスの反射率は基準値以下です。

11 形状
Form

建物形状は敷地形状や機能などと密接に関係している（Form follows function：形態は機能に従う）ため、その関係性を明確な英語表現で伝えることで、受け取る側も理解できます。

examples

▶ The building outline is formed by the way direction of the site and its surroundings.
建物外形は敷地周囲の動線によって形作られる。

▶ The advertising panels along the passageway are a rectangular shape.
通路に掲示される広告用パネルは長方形となっております。

▶ The latest toilet cubicles have a curved sliding door for wheelchair users.
最新の個室トイレには車いす対応の曲面引き戸を採用しております。

▶ The triangular-shaped site is used as a communal space for neighbors.
三角形の敷地は近隣の共用空間として使われます。

▶ The exhibiting corridor has waved walls on both sides.
展示廊下は両面に波打つ壁があります。

▶ The three-dimensional tilted external wall is the feature of this restaurant.
斜めに傾いた3次元の外壁が、このレストランの特徴です。

🍷 Quick Chat ｜呟嗟のひとこと

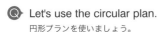 Let's use the circular plan.
円形プランを使いましょう。

key phrases

be formed by~
〜によって形づけられる。
The building's shape is formed by the user's action.
建物の形は利用者の行動によって形成される。

way direction
動線
The way direction should be simple in public transport buildings.
公共交通施設の動線はシンプルでなければならない。

along~
〜に沿って。通路や敷地境界に沿って、の時に使う。類似表現に alongside。
The site is located alongside the river.
敷地は川に沿っている。

rectangular/triangular
四角形（長方形）の／三角形の。もっと簡単に rectangle/triangle と表現することもある。形状を表す単語には他に oval 楕円形の、circular 円形の、polygon 多角形の、geometrical 幾何学的な、などがある。

neighbor
隣人、隣の人、近隣住民。似た表現で people nextdoor がある。

on both sides
両側に、両面に。面は sides と複数形となる。ちなみに両面テープは double-sided tape。
The walkway has trees on both sides.
遊歩道の両側には木々がある。

---

vocabulary

building outline 建物外形	wheelchair user 車いす利用者
advertising panel 広告用パネル、看板	corridor 廊下
passageway 通路	waved 波打った
latest 最新の	feature 特徴
toilet cubicle 個室トイレ	circular 円形の
curved 曲がった、カーブした	oval 楕円形の
sliding door 引き戸	polygon 多角形の

 No, it would be difficult to use.
いや、使いづらいでしょう。

12 状態
Situation/Condition(of the site)

状態の表現には抽象的なものが多いため日本語のニュアンスそのままでは通じにくいことがあります。まず、抽象的な日本語を具体的な日本語に"翻訳"するなど、最初は多少説明的になりつつも、丁寧に伝えていくよう心がけましょう。

examples

- The artworks dotted around the park give a refreshing impression to visitors.
  公園に散りばめられたアート作品が訪問者にさわやかな印象を与えます。

- In comparison to Europeans, Asians recognize beauty in chaos.
  欧州人と比較して、アジア人は混沌の美しさを理解します。

- The space demonstrates complexity rather than disorder.
  この空間は混沌よりも複雑性を演出します。

- Each volume is a different size, but centered on the same line.
  それぞれボリュームは違う大きさですが、中心を同一線上に配置しています。

- The cafe within the entrance hall not only has a cheerful atmosphere but also attracts customers.
  玄関ホール内にあるカフェは賑わいだけでなく集客性もある。

- The reference corner was designed to be a comfortable space with plenty of natural light.
  閲覧コーナーはたくさんの自然光を取り込むことで心地よい空間をデザインしました。

💡 Quick Chat | 咄嗟のひとこと

Q Wouldn't this plan cause a congestion of passengers?
このプランでは通行人は混雑しませんか？

key phrases

dotted around~
~に散りばめられた

in comparison to~
~と比較して、~と比べれば。動詞は compare。
After comparing prices, we are happy to use this material.
価格を比べれば、私たちは喜んでこの建材を使います。

recognize beauty in~
~に美しさを見出す、~に美しさを感じる、~の美しさを理解する

rather than~
~よりむしろ。rather が付くことで「むしろ」というニュアンスになる。

center on~
~を中心にする。center〔名詞〕真ん中、〔動詞〕集中する、真ん中に集める。

attracts customers
多くの集客ができる、集客性がある

plenty of natural light
ふんだんな自然光

vocabulary

dotted 散りばめられた	disorder 混沌
refreshing impression さわやかな印象	cheerful atmosphere 賑わい
visitors 訪問者、来客者	reference corner 閲覧コーナー
demonstrate 演出する、行動する	comfortable 心地よい、快適な
complexity 複雑性	plenty 十分
	congestion 混雑

 No, the passenger flows don't cross each other.
いえ、それぞれの動線は交錯しません。

13 個人住宅
Private House

個人住宅を考える時にはまず日本と海外の住環境の違いを理解する必要があります。日本の住宅は新築の戸建て信仰が一般的ですが、景観保全に努めている国や地域では古い建築物を改修して住み続ける場合が多くあります。

examples

▶ A smaller site makes for a simpler residential interior.
より小さな敷地では住宅のインテリアもよりシンプルになる。

▶ The second house is situated near a natural hot spring in a rural area.
別荘は地方の天然温泉の湧き出る場所に位置している。

▶ The residence has some windows that stretch from floor to ceiling because it is in a suburban district.
この住宅は郊外にあるため、床から天井まで広がる窓がいくつかあります。

▶ The vacation villa is situated by the lake so that it has good views.
別荘は湖畔にある眺めの良い場所に位置しています。

▶ A site surrounded by silver birch trees at the bottom of a mountain was proposed for the country house.
その別荘は山のふもとの白樺に囲まれた敷地に提案されました。

💡 Quick Chat | 咄嗟のひとこと

Q: What is the client's first priority?
施主の第一の要望は？

key phrases

make for~
～を促進する、～を促す

be situated near~
～の近くに位置する。situate〔動詞〕場所を定める。situation〔名詞〕状況、状態、場所。
The weekend house is situated near the hill.
週末に滞在する家は丘の近くに位置しています。

from floor to ceiling
床から天井まで。窓、開口部、もしくは内装などで部屋の壁面の高さ目一杯活用する際に用いる。

because~
～の理由で。because の後は文章が続くが、because of の後には名詞が続く。

so that~
～するために

surrounded by~
～によって囲まれている。敷地周辺や建物周辺の状況を説明するのに便利な用語。

at the bottom of a mountain
山のふもとにて。bottom には「底」と同時に「ふもと」などの意味もある。反対語に at the top of a mountain 頂上にて。

be proposed for~
～に対して提案される。proposal 提案。

---

vocabulary

simple シンプルな、単純な	**vacation villa** 別荘
natural hot spring 天然温泉	**silver birch** 白樺
rural area 田舎の地域	**country house** 別荘
stretch 伸びる、広がる	**first priority** 第一の希望、最優先
suburban district 郊外の地域	**whole family** 家族全員

 It's the living room where the whole family can gather.
家族全員が集える大きな居間です。

14 集合住宅
Housing Complex

集合住宅も日本と海外それぞれに異なる環境下で計画されます。厳しい規制の中で決められる高層建築物の説明はもちろんのこと、廊下、住戸プランなどの関係性の説明が求められます。

examples

- ▶ The mansion was built to the maximum height limit permitted on the site.
  このマンションは敷地に許された高さ制限の目いっぱいまで建てられました。

- ▶ The condominium apartment building with south facing rooms is a one-side corridor type.
  南向き住戸の分譲住宅棟は片廊下型です。

- ▶ An east and west facing room layout plan makes a difference in terms of the amount of sunshine received.
  東と西に向いた住戸プランだと日当たりに差が出ます。

- ▶ An urban rental apartment for single people requires differentiation from other apartment types by its design.
  都心の単身者向け賃貸マンションにはデザインによる差別化が必要です。

- ▶ Family apartments in suburban areas give importance to spaciousness, air flow and affordability.
  郊外のファミリー向けマンションには広さと通風、そして手頃な価格を重視しました。

- ▶ The layout of the common space in a shared house is a key factor.
  シェアハウスは共用空間の配置がカギとなります。

🍷 Quick Chat ｜ 咄嗟のひとこと

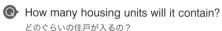
- How many housing units will it contain?
  どのぐらいの住戸が入るの？

key phrases

be built to~
～まで建てられる。built は build（建てる）の過去・過去分詞形。

maximum height limit
高さ制限いっぱいの

south facing room
南向きの部屋。face〔動詞〕向く。

one-side corridor type
片廊下型。似た表現で balcony type がある。中廊下型は internal corridor type。
Let's set out the advantages and disadvantages of an internal-corridor type apartment.
中廊下型アパートのメリット・デメリットを挙げてみましょう。

make a difference
違いを生み出す。差が生まれる。make no difference 違いはない。
We make no difference between plan A and plan B.
プラン A とプラン B に違いはありません。

in terms of~
～において、～について

give importance to~
～を重視する

---

vocabulary

mansion　マンション、集合住宅	family apartment　ファミリー向けマンション
height limit　高さ制限	
permitted　許可された、認められた	spaciousness　広さ
condominium apartment　分譲アパート	air flow　風通し
	affordability　手頃な価格
amount　量	shared house　シェアハウス
sunshine received　日当たり	key factor　重要項目、鍵

 Twenty-four units.
24 戸です。

15 オフィス
Office

オフィス空間をデザインするときにはその国や地域の働き方に配慮しなければなりません。給湯室や印刷室などの機能名称は対訳がありますが、それらの配置や関係性、そしてその意味合いは丁寧に説明する必要があります。

examples

- ▶ The floor is dotted with a number of meeting spaces.
  たくさんの打ち合わせスペースがフロアに点在している。

- ▶ Personal desks should occupy slightly hidden spaces to increase work efficiency.
  個人のデスクは集中できるように少し隠れた場所にすべきです。

- ▶ Free-address office layouts require personal belongings to be limited to a minimum amount.
  フリーアドレス方式のオフィスレイアウトは個人の持ち物が最小限である必要があります。

- ▶ The white board finish wall can be used as a projection screen.
  ホワイトボード仕様の壁はプロジェクターのスクリーンとしても活用できます。

- ▶ With these cores layout, is the rentable floor area ratio of this floor sufficient?
  このコアレイアウトでこの階のレンタブル比は十分ですか？

- ▶ The reception area should be comfortable for visitors.
  受付スペースは来訪者にとって心地よい空間であるべきです。

💡 Quick Chat ｜咄嗟のひとこと

- Where will the smoking area go?
  喫煙所はどこに置きますか？

key phrases

be dotted with~
~が点在している。dot〔名詞〕点、〔動詞〕点在する。過去形・過去分詞形は dotted であり、点線は dotted line。

slightly
少しばかり。slight〔形容詞〕少しの、僅かな。
A slight draught runs through the room.
僅かな隙間風が通り抜ける。

increase work efficiency
仕事の効率を上げる

personal belongings
個人の所有物。belong〔動詞〕所有する。belongings〔名詞〕所有物。似た表現で personal stuff がある。

rentable floor area ratio
レンタブル比。GFA:Gross Floor Area 延床面積、NRA:Net Rentable Area: 総賃貸可能面積、Occupied area: 専有面積、Site area: 敷地面積。

at the end of~
~の端に。~の終わりに。部屋の奥、廊下の奥、フロアの奥について表現する際に使える。
The ventilation opening is required at the end of corridor.
換気の開口部が廊下の端に求められている。

---

vocabulary

occupy 占める、位置する	belonging 所有物
hidden 隠れた	limited 限られた
require 求める	minimum amount 最小限の量
personal 個人の	projection screen 投影スクリーン

 It will go at the end of the floor.
フロアの端です。

16 公共建築
Public Building

最近の公共建築には複合的な機能が求められています。それらは既存の建築タイプで分類できるものではなく、なるべく具体的な用途を説明することが求められます。

---

examples

- ▶ In an era of e-books, libraries may need to consider ideas like the inclusion of cafe spaces.
  電子書籍時代の図書館はカフェを併設するようなアイデアが必要となるかも知れません。

- ▶ Commercial spaces in station buildings transform commuters into customers.
  駅舎内に商業施設を作ることで、通勤者を消費者に変えた。

- ▶ Government offices in the future must not only serve an administrative role but also function as gathering spaces for citizens.
  これからの役所は業務だけではなく、市民が集える場所でなければならない。

- ▶ Old public facilities can be further utilized by making them barrier-free.
  バリアフリー化することで古い公共施設でもさらに使い続けられます。

- ▶ The complex facility requires a clear sign plan.
  複合施設は明快なサイン計画が求められます。

Quick Chat | 咄嗟のひとこと

- Do you have experience of working on public building projects?
  公共建築のプロジェクトに従事した経験はありますか？

key phrases

ideas like~
〜のようなアイデア

inclusion of~
〜の併設。inclusion〔名詞〕含めること、組み入れること。

transform A into B
AをBに変える。建築的な表現にrefurbishやrenovateなどもある。renovate A into B. The apartment building will be renovated into a hostel.
アパートを宿泊施設に改修する。

not only A but also B
AだけでなくBも。似た表現でA as well as Bがある。A、B両方とも。関連してeither A or B. AとBのどちらか、neither A nor B. AとBどちらでもない。

for citizens
市民のための

make ~ barrier-free
〜をバリアフリー化する。バリアフリーはカタカナ英語として親しまれているが、同様の意味でstep-freeもある。freeには「なし」という意味があり、例えば禁煙はsmoke-freeとなる。gender-free 男女平等。

---

vocabulary

era	時代	gathering space	集まる場所
e-book	電子書籍	citizen	市民
commuter	通勤者	further	さらに
customer	お客	utilize	利用する
government office	役所	clear	明快な
administrative role	業務	sign plan	サイン計画

 Yes, I gained such experience in my previous office.
はい、以前勤務していた会社で経験があります。

17 公共空間
Public Space

「図」としての建物だけでなく、「地」としての広場や道路などを意識的に計画に組み込むことも、建築計画には求められます。都市計画の視点から公共空間を考え、きちんと説明することで、建物の提案が説得力を持ちます。

examples

- ▶ From the perspective of urban planning, a part of this project site should be made into a public square.
  都市計画の観点から、この敷地の一部は公共の広場とすべきです。

- ▶ The number of vehicles around the station should be restricted.
  駅周辺の車の量は制限すべきだ。

- ▶ Using squares in London as a reference, the rest spaces are located randomly in the office.
  ロンドンの広場を参照にし、職場に休憩所をランダムに点在させます。

- ▶ We agree with the introduction of rental cycles to improve air pollution.
  大気汚染改善のためにレンタル自転車の導入に同意します。

- ▶ The cycle path will be upgraded at the same time.
  自転車道も同時に改善されるでしょう。

- ▶ It is the most effective way to commercialize spaces under the rail tracks.
  電車の高架下を商業化させるのは最も効果的な方法です。

💡 *Quick Chat* | 咄嗟のひとこと

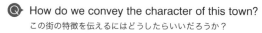

- ❓ How do we convey the character of this town?
  この街の特徴を伝えるにはどうしたらいいだろうか？

key phrases

from the perspective of~
〜の観点から

should be~
〜するべきだ

be restricted
制限される。be limited も同義。
Access to the communal garden is limited to neighbors.
共用庭へのアクセスは近隣住民だけに制限されている。

use~as a reference
〜を参照する

be upgraded
改善される。be improved も同義。
The traffic conjestion will be impoved by this road layout plan.
交通渋滞はこの道路配置計画によって改善されるでしょう。

the most effective way to~
〜は最も効果的な方法。「効果的な方法」の似た表現には efficient method など。
The inclusion of a square in a business district is the most effective way to reduce office workers' stress.
ビジネス街に広場を導入することは、オフィスで働く人のストレスを減らすのに最も効果的な方法です。

vocabulary

urban planning 都市計画	rental cycle レンタル自転車
public square 公共の広場	improve 改善する
vehicle 車	air pollution 大気汚染
restricted 制限された	cycle path 自転車道
reference 参照	at the same time 同時に
rest space 休憩所	commercialize 商業化する
introduction 導入	under the rail tracks 高架下

Step 1　Conveying Design Ideas　デザインの魅力を伝える

Ⓐ　Why don't we describe the building and public square by using different colors?　公共の広場と建物を色分けして描いてはどうだろうか？

18 商業施設①(小規模〜中規模店舗)
Commercial Building (small to medium scale)

小規模の商業施設は広告的な役割を担うため、大胆なデザインを盛り込む機会になります。それゆえ、具体的なコンセプトを明確に伝える必要があります。

examples

- ▶ The motor van was modified into a take-out lunch box shop.
  トラックをテイクアウト弁当のお店へ改装した。

- ▶ Smoked glass was used for the facade of the cafe space to provide privacy in the internal space.
  カフェのファサードには内部への人目を避けて曇りガラスを採用しました。

- ▶ The interior of a fashion retailer requires a showy design like that of an advertisement.
  ファッション店の内装は広告のような派手なデザインが求められる。

- ▶ The bare skeleton interior might better enhance the displayed products.
  躯体むき出しの内装が展示商品自体を引き立たせるかもしれません。

- ▶ The circulation of staff between the kitchen and dining area shouldn't interfere with that of the guests.
  厨房と客席への従業員の動線がお客様の動線を妨げるべきではありません。

- ▶ This is a standing bar resembling an English pub where you can have a quick drink after work.
  これは仕事上がりにちょっと一杯引っ掛ける立ち飲み屋、いわばイングリッシュパブのような店です。

💡 Quick Chat | 咄嗟のひとこと

Q How much time do we have to finish the interior work?
内装工事に掛けられる時間は？

key phrases

be modified into~
～へ改装された
The floor layout was modified to cater to smaller tenants.
フロアの配置計画はより小さなテナントのために改装された。

take-out
持ち帰り。take away と言うこともある。
The shop front has a window for take-out customers.
店先には持ち帰り客用の窓がある。

smoked glass
曇りガラス。同じ製品を frosted glass と呼ぶこともある。網入り防犯ガラスは wired safety glass。

require
求める。request〔名詞〕要求、リクエスト。
Cost effectiveness is required for the shop interior.
お店の内装は費用対効果が求められています。

bare skeleton interior
躯体むき出しの内装。bare には裸の意味がある。
He is addicted to using bare concrete walls.
彼はむき出しのコンクリート壁を使うことにはまっている。

quick drink after work
仕事上がりの"軽い"一杯
Shall we have a quick drink?
軽く一杯やらない?

vocabulary

motor van	トラック	advertisement	広告
modify	改装する	bare skeleton	むき出しの躯体
take-out	持ち帰り、テイクアウト	enhance	引き立たせる、高める、増す
smoked glass	曇りガラス	circulation	動線
provide	備える、提供する	interfere	妨げる
internal	内側の	pub	パブ、酒場
retailer	お店	cater	提供する
showy	派手な	cost effectiveness	費用対効果

 About three weeks.
大体3週間です。

19 商業施設② （複合商業施設）
Commercial Building(complex type)

規模の大きな商業施設では、施設内の機能名称とその位置関係を適切に説明する必要があります。日本のデパートのような商業施設では中層〜高層ビルが多くみられますが、欧米の商業施設では低層かつ広大な建物面積の建築が多くみられます。

examples

- The cafe beside the hotel reception is for customers from outside as well.
  ホテルのレセプションに併設するカフェは外部からの訪問客用でもあります。

- In Japan, popular art galleries used to occupy the top floors of department stores, serving a cultural role.
  日本では人気のある美術館はかつてデパート最上階にあり、文化的役割を担っていました。

- The music auditorium has been designed to go at the top of the building.
  音楽堂ホールが建物の最上階に計画されました。

- Theater complex buildings are suitable for station fronts, where many potential customers pass by.
  映画館併設の複合商業施設は潜在的な訪問客が多く通る駅前が相応しい。

- A food court is on the ground floor allowing easy access by customers.
  フードコートはお客様が気軽に立ち寄れるよう地上階にあります。

Quick Chat ｜咄嗟のひとこと

Q: How do we promote consumption behavior?
消費行動を促すにはどのようにしたらよいか？

key phrases

beside~
〜のそばに。〜に併設された。似た表現で adjacent to〜 がある。
The family type hotel is located adjacent to the theme park.
家族向けホテルがテーマパークに隣接してある。

hotel reception
ホテルの受付。reception area のように人々が溜る場所には lobby や hall や foyer（ホワイエ）などがある。

~as well
〜もまた、〜でもある

used to~
かつては〜していた

occupy (the top floors)
（最上階に）位置する、占める

be designed to go at~
〜の位置に計画された

be suitable for~
〜に相応しい。〜に合っている
A shopping space is suitable for the inside of the station.
商業空間は駅の中にふさわしい。

where potential customers pass by
潜在顧客が通る場所

allowing easy access
気軽に立ち寄れるように

---

vocabulary

reception　受付
serve　役にたつ、役割を持つ
auditorium　音楽堂
theater complex　映画館併設の
station front　駅前
potential　可能性のある、潜在的な
pass by　通りすぎる
consumption behavior　消費行動

 We need an idea that makes customers stay longer.
訪問客の滞在時間を長くする仕掛けが必要だ。

20 建築テーマ① （ローコスト）
Low-cost Architecture

世界中どこでもコスト削減は建築プロジェクトの鍵となります。日本のシンプルなデザインにはローコスト建築の工夫があります。どのようにしてコストを削減、抑えているのかを丁寧に説明しましょう。

examples

▶ With a limited budget, we should make clear priorities.
限られた予算では優先事項を明確にすべきです。

▶ First of all, let's make sure it is earthquake-proof and heat-proof.
まず、耐震性と耐熱性を確認しましょう。

▶ We might reduce the construction costs if we eliminate the finishing materials.
もし仕上げ材を省けば施工費を削減できるかもしれません。

▶ Contrarily, it might cost more to refurbish the existing buildings.
逆に、既存建築を改修することでコストがかさむ場合もあります。

▶ Comfort of living may be sacrificed if you pursue cost effectiveness too much.
もし費用対効果を追求しすぎると住み心地が犠牲になるかもしれません。

▶ There is a construction method involving prefabrication in the factory and assemblage on site.
工場で事前に施工をし、現場で組み立てる施工方法もあります。

🍷 Quick Chat ｜咄嗟のひとこと

❓ What is most important in this limited budget?
この限られた予算の中で何が一番大切ですか？

key phrases

limited budget
限られた予算。逆に無限の予算は unlimited budget となる。
Sometimes, a limited budget creates good architecture.
ときに、限られた予算が良い建築を生み出す。

reduce the cost
コストを削減する。似た表現として cut down the cost.

construction cost
施工費、建築費、工事費、建設費。Builders' cost 建設作業員コスト、人工。
The builders' cost is getting higher and higher.
建設の人件費はどんどん高くなっている。

cost more
多くコストがかかる、費用がかさむ。cost much more コストがもっと多くかかる。反対語は cost less。
Better products might cost more.
より良い製品とはコストもよりかかる。

sacrifice the comfort of living
住み心地を犠牲にする

assemblage on site
現場での組み立て。プレハブとは逆の施工方法のこと。assemble 組み立てる。
This product was designed in my country and assembled in Southeast Asia.
この商品は私の国でデザインされ、東南アジアで組み立てられた。

---

vocabulary

budget 予算	contrarily 逆に
first of all まず、最初に	refurbish 改修する
let's〜 〜しよう	existing building 既存建物
make sure 確認する	sacrifice 犠牲にする
priority 優先、優先事項	pursue 追求する
earthquake-proof 耐震性のある	effectiveness 効果、効率
heat-proof 耐熱性	construction method 施工方法
eliminate 排除する、省く	prefabrication 組み立て式、プレハブ
finishing material 仕上げ材	assemblage 組み立て

 Privacy.
プライバシーの確保です。

21 建築テーマ②(エコ・サステイナブル)
Ecological/Sustainable Architecture

21世紀に入り、先進国は低成長社会を迎え、持続可能な建築環境を生み出すことが求められています。日本の技術力を駆使した環境負荷低減を採用するには、相手にそのメリットが伝わるようにきちんと説明します。

examples

- **Installing solar energy generation panels on the roof helps to save energy.**
  屋根に太陽光発電パネルを設置することで省エネルギー化に寄与しています。

- **The horizontal louvers on the southern facade have a shielding effect against direct sunlight.**
  南側ファサードに水平ルーバーを設置することは直射日光の遮蔽効果があります。

- **It aims to reduce the load of ventilation with a natural air-flow system in the house.**
  住宅内の自然換気を促すことで換気負荷の低減を目指します。

- **Sustainability should be considered in the design of the building.**
  建物のデザインは持続可能性を考慮したものでなければならない。

- **The reason why we adopted a roof top garden is not only for its designability, but also to make the building eco-friendly.**
  屋上緑化を採用した理由はデザイン性だけでなく、環境に優しい建築を目指したからです。

💡 Quick Chat | 咄嗟のひとこと

Q How much do we reduce the environmental impact by adopting roof greening?　屋上緑化を採用することでどれくらい環境への影響を低減できるのか？

key phrases

horizontal louver
水平ルーバー。垂直ルーバーは vertical louver.

shielding effect against~
～に対する遮蔽効果

direct sunlight
直射日光。間接日射は indirect sunlight.

The parallel louvers on the south facade protect the internal environment from direct sunlight.
南側立面の水平ルーバーは室内環境を直射日光から守る。

reduce the load of~
～の負荷を低減する

The insulation between walls reduces the heat from outside.
壁の間にある断熱材は外部からの熱を軽減する。

the reason why~
～と言う理由で。似た意味で because もある。

eco-friendly
環境に優しい。-friendly は～に優しい、という接尾語。user-friendly 利用者に優しい。planet-friendly 地球に優しい。

---

vocabulary

install　設置する
solar energy generation panel　太陽光発電パネル
saving energy　省エネルギー
horizontal　水平の
louvers　ルーバー、ガラリ、日除け
shielding　遮蔽
effect　効果
against　対して
direct sunlight　直射日光

aim　目指す
load　負荷
ventilation　換気
natural air-flow system　自然換気
sustainability　持続可能性
consider　考慮する
adopt　採用する
eco-friendly　環境に優しい
roughly　だいたい

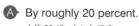 By roughly 20 percent.
大体 20 パーセントです。

建築テーマ③（リノベーション）
Renovation/Refurbishment

既存建築を改修し使い続けるリノベーションという考え方が日本でも取り入れられています。しかし、手間と費用を考えた時に新築を選択した方が良いのではないかという議論も起きます。その建築が生み出した時間や街並みの保全など社会に与える影響も含め、丁寧に説明する必要があります。

examples

▶ The planning of houses needs ideas for extension and reduction in accordance with the transformation of family members.
住宅計画には家族の変化に合わせて増減築する考え方が求められている。

▶ Even if the empty building is renovated, there should be a business plan for its future use.
たとえその空き物件をリノベーションしても、後の事業計画が無ければならない。

▶ The key factor in two-generation family houses is the clear division between shared and private space.
二世代住居で大切な要素は共有部分と専有部分を明確に分けることです。

▶ It might require time and money to refurbish the empty house.
空き家を改修するには費用と時間が必要かもしれません。

▶ For renovation projects, we start by examining to what extent the building is earthquake-proof.
改修計画では、私たちは耐震性能を検討することから始める。

Quick Chat | 咄嗟のひとこと

Q. How old is this building?
この建築は築何年ですか？

key phrases

in accordance with~
〜に応じて

even if~
たとえ〜でも。似た表現に although や though がある。
We should choose this material even if it costs more.
私たちはたとえコストが多くかかってもこの建材を選ぶべきです。

two-generation family
二世代家族。three-generation family 三世代家族。

require time and money
時間と費用がかかる

examine to what extent~
どの程度〜かを検証する。性能を表すには specification も用いられる。
It might take more time to examine the original specifications of this building.
この建物の最初の性能を検証するとなると、より多くの時間がかかるかもしれない。

---

vocabulary

extension　増築	refurbish　改修する
reduction　減築	empty house　空き家
renovate　改修する	examine　検討する、検証する、試験する
business　ビジネスの	earthquake-proof　耐震性のある
shared space　共有部分	specification　性能
private space　専有部分	

 It is about thirty-five years old.
およそ築35年です。

部屋の機能
Function

提案する部屋を説明するとき、その機能だけでなく、メンテナンスなど配慮すべき点も同時に説明できればより説得力が増します。

examples

- ▶ The living space that gets a lot of sunshine is situated on the south side and the wet area on the north.
  日当たりのいいリビングは南側に、水回りは北側に配置します。

- ▶ The bathroom has ventilation to prevent mold.
  風呂場はカビ防止のため換気が取れるようにします。

- ▶ The materials used for the office interior are a lighter color.
  オフィス内装に使用した建築素材はより明るい色とします。

- ▶ The stair risers shouldn't be applied to the landing to allow for universal design.
  ユニバーサルデザインのために蹴上げを踊り場に設けるべきではない。

🍷 Quick Chat ｜咄嗟のひとこと

- What is a *tokonoma*?
  床の間ってなんですか？

key phrases

situate on~
～に配置する。situation〔名詞〕位置、状況。
The entrance space is situated on the north side corner.
玄関空間は北側角に配置している。

wet area
水回り。台所・浴室・便所など、水を使う場所。
The wet area is usually arranged on the north side.
水回りは通常、北側にまとめられる。

prevent mold
カビを防止する。mold-proof 防カビ。mold-proof paint 防カビペンキ。
The bath room wall is painted with mold-proof paint.
浴室の壁は防カビペンキで塗られている。

a lighter color
より明るい色の

allow for~
～を考慮する

for universal design
ユニバーサルデザインのために
A slip-resistant material and contrasting color are used on the corridor floor for universal design.
廊下の床では滑り止めの建材と対比色がユニバーサルデザインのために使われている。

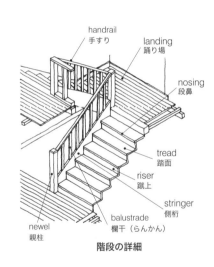

階段の詳細

---

vocabulary

situate 置く、場所を定める	stair riser 階段の蹴上
wet area 水回り	landing 踊り場
bathroom 風呂場	universal design ユニバーサルデザイン（利用者の差異・能力を問わず利用できるデザイン）
ventilation 換気	
prevent 防ぐ	
mold カビ	
material 材質、建材	

Ⓐ It is the special corner in the guest room where flowers and pictures are displayed. 客間に設ける特別な一角で絵や花を飾ります。

平面計画

Planning

平面計画は方位、敷地周辺、隣室などとの関係性とともに丁寧に説明できれば、受け取る側もイメージしやすくなります。

examples

▶ We prepared three different plans in anticipation of various situations.
様々な使用状況を想定し、3つの異なる平面計画を用意しました。

▶ The living space is planned in the center of the house.
この住宅では居間が中心に計画されます。

▶ This art museum has a spiral floor plan that allows visitors to follow the artists' history along the wall.
この美術館はらせん状の平面計画とし、来館者は壁に沿って作家の変遷を追えます。

▶ Although the flat is for a two-generation family, the plan keeps their privacy.
この住戸は二世代家族向けでありながら、プライバシーを確保した間取りです。

▶ The glass facade of the building shows the user's activity.
建物のガラスファサードは利用者の活動の様子を見せます。

▶ We feel a sense of boundary with *shoji*, a partition that uses Japanese paper.
私たちには和紙を使った仕切りである障子を境界とみなす感性があります。

Quick Chat | 咄嗟のひとこと

Q What is the plan of this housing unit?
この住戸の間取りは？

key phrases

prepare
準備する。prepare for~/ ~に備える、~に向けて準備する。
Three drawing sets should be prepared for the meeting with the client this afternoon.
午後の施主打ち合わせ用に図面を3セット準備しなければならない。

in various situations
様々な状況で。似たような表現では in various circumstances。
The housing plan is designed to match various circumstances.
住戸計画はいくつかの状況に合わせてデザインされている。

in the center of~
~の中心に。in the middle of~/ ~の真ん中に
The courtyard is located in the middle of geometric volumes.
中庭は幾何学ボリュームの真ん中に位置している。

along the wall
壁に沿って。along the river 川に沿って。
The main corridor is planned along the auditoriums.
主廊下は音楽堂群に沿っている。

although~
~ではあるが。似たような意味では even though もしくは though。
Though the planned number of visitors is small, the main reception is spaciously designed.
訪問者の想定数は小さいが、受付は大きく設計した。

住宅の間どり例

vocabulary

prepare 準備する	although ~ではあるが
anticipation 想定	two-generation family 二世代家族
various 様々な	plan 間取り
situation 状況	sense 感覚、感性
spiral らせん	boundary 境界
along~ ~に沿って	Japanese paper 和紙

A. It is a flat with two bedrooms, a combination living-dining room and kitchen. 2LDKです。

動線・シークエンス
Circulation/Sequence

動線は住宅内の単純なものから、公共施設の複雑なものまであります。明快な空間構成による建築は動線も自ずとシンプルになるはずです。説明もシンプルを目指しましょう。

examples

- ▶ The exhibition space and back of house are clearly separated.
  展示スペースと管理エリアは明確に分離しました。

- ▶ The evacuation route isn't congested.
  避難経路は混雑していません。

- ▶ It is hard for foreign tourists to immediately recognize the sign amidst the flow of commuters.
  通勤者の流れのなかで、外国人観光客が案内板を一瞬で識別するのは難しい。

- ▶ The paths of family members pass through the living room.
  家族の動線は居間を通過します。

- ▶ The circulation to each of the auditoriums has been shortened.
  それぞれの音楽堂にアクセスする動線は短くしました。

- ▶ The circulation between the kitchen and laundry space is short in this house.
  この住宅の台所から洗濯場への動線は短い。

💡 Quick Chat | 咄嗟のひとこと

- ❓ Why is the circulation so long?
  なぜ動線がそのように長いのでしょうか？

key phrases

back of house
管理エリア。時に B.O.H. と略される。backyard などとも呼ばれる。「家の裏」と言う意味から、施設などの従業員エリアのことを差す。

Security at the door to back of house area should be restricted.
管理部門への扉の防犯はしっかりしていなければならない。

evacuation route
避難経路。escape route 等の呼び方もある。関連語に evacuation space 避難場所。

A wide evacuation space is required around the stadium.
競技場の周辺には十分な避難場所が求められている。

be congested
混雑した。be jammed も同様の表現。関連語に交通渋滞 traffic congestion や traffic jam。

Street layouts should pay consideration to traffic jams.
道路のレイアウトは交通渋滞を考慮していなければならない。

it is hard for A to B
AにとってBすることは難しい。hard には硬いという意味と同時に難しいという意味もある。同様の表現に it is difficult for … to がある。

amidst the flow of commuters
通勤者の流れの中で。commuter 通勤者。commute 通勤する。

The architects working on this transport facility project should be required to experience commuting there.
この交通施設計画に関わる建築家はそこでの通勤経験が求められる。

shorten
短くする。shorten は short の動詞。関連語に widen 広げる。

The boulevard can be widened so that many vehicles can pass.
大通りはたくさんの車を通すために広げられる。

---

vocabulary

clearly 明確に	recognize 認識する、気づく
separate 分ける	sign サイン、標識
evacuation 避難	amidst~ ～の中で
route/circulation/path 経路、動線	commuter 通勤者
congested 混雑した	showcase 見せる、目立たせる
immediately すぐさま	

 Because it has the function of showcasing the beautiful landscape.
なぜなら、美しい景色を見せる役割があるからです。

26 眺望
View

建物からの眺望、特に日本の景観には特別な説明が求められます。海や山に囲まれた日本の自然環境はもちろんのこと、都心部の密集地に建つ建築物など海外の人からどのように見えるのかを相手側に立って説明する必要があります。

examples

- ▶ The owner can see the blue sky through a skylight.
  オーナーは天窓を通して青空を見ることができます。

- ▶ The windows were arranged to avoid the surrounding electricity poles.
  窓は周辺の電柱を避けるように決められました。

- ▶ Visitors can enjoy the panoramic view of mountains from the large-sized window stretching the whole facade.
  訪問者は全面開口窓から望む山々のパノラマビューが楽しめます。

- ▶ The balcony looks toward the bay area.
  バルコニーは湾岸地域に向いている。

- ▶ The opening was planned in accordance with the movement of the sun.
  太陽の動きに合わせて開口部は計画されました。

- ▶ Despite many obstructions around the site, the positioning of the windows was well coordinated.
  敷地周辺にはたくさんの障害物があるが、窓の位置はきちんと調整されていました。

Quick Chat | 咄嗟のひとこと

This is a residential dense area, right?
この地域は住宅密集地ですよね？

key phrases

see A through B
Bを通じてAを見る

a view of~
〜の景色。a unique view of the site その敷地ならでは景色。
Each room has a view of the sunset over the sea.
それぞれの部屋から海に沈む夕焼けが見える。

look toward(s)~
〜に向いている
This picture is of the view looking towards south.
この写真は南向きの景色です。

movement of the sun
太陽の動き

despite~
〜にも関わらず。似た表現に regardless of~、nonetheless~。
Despite facing north, the site contains a vast field.
北向きだが、敷地には広大な野原が広がる。

positioning of~
〜の配置

---

vocabulary

owner オーナー、所有者	balcony バルコニー
skylight 天窓	toward(s)~ 〜に向かって
avoid 避ける	despite~ 〜にも関わらず
electricity pole 電柱	obstruction 障害物
panoramic パノラマ式の、全景の見える	well coordinated きちんと調整された
	nonetheless~ 〜にも関わらず
whole 全体	

 Yes, but we have a good view from the roof top.
はい、しかし屋上からの眺望があります。

27 開口部
Opening

開口部の説明をするときに、その大きさ、方位だけでなく周辺環境なども説明する必要があります。自然豊かな環境はもちろんのこと、日本特有の都市部の環境などは詳細に説明する必要があります。

examples

- The tall window stretching from floor to ceiling gains enough daylight even in winter time.
  床から天井までの窓は冬季でも十分な採光が得られます。

- This window connects the view between the interior and exterior.
  窓は内部と外部の視線を繋げる。

- We agree that the windows are your design. But did you also think about the privacy of the residents?
  窓はあなたのデザインであるのは理解できます。しかし住み手のプライバシーは考えましたか？

- At the same time, we have to consider how to reduce the load of the air-conditioning for the large windows.
  同時に私たちは大きな窓のためにどのように空調負荷を低減するか考慮しなければならない。

- People can easily gather near the window.
  窓辺に人は集まりやすい。

- Although the window is tiny, it has a special design because we studied its location and size.
  窓は小さいながらも、位置とサイズを検討したので、特別なデザインとなりました。

💬 Quick Chat ｜咄嗟のひとこと

Q Is there an opening on the north side?
　　北側に開口部はありますか？

key phrases

from floor to ceiling
床から天井まで。window stretching from floor to ceiling の類似表現に full height window 全面開口部。

gain daylight
昼間の採光を得る

between A and B
A と B の間。connection from A to B は A から B へのつながり。

agree that~
～に同意する。agree with~/ ～に賛成する。反対語は disagree 同意しない。

think about~
～について考える。about を忘れやすいので要注意。類似表現に think of~/ ～を考える。ほぼ同じ意味だが、think about はもう少し時間をかけて考える場合に使う。

Our team members can think of alternative ideas in a short period of time.
チームメンバーは短い時間で対案を考えることができる。

at the same time
同時に。似た表現に at once や in the meantime がある。

The front window and back door should be opened at the same time to allow the circulation of fresh air.
前面窓と勝手口ドアは新鮮な空気を得るために同時に開け放たれなければならない。

consider~
～を考慮する。似た表現に think about~ がある。

Sunlight should be considered when designing the window openings.
窓開口部をデザインするときは日照を考慮しなければならない。

---

vocabulary

gain	得る	resident	住民
enough	十分な	load	負荷
connect	繋ぐ	air-conditioning	空調
agree	同意する	gather	集まる
privacy	プライバシー		

A No, because of the neighbors.
いいえ。隣の家があるからです。

窓
Window

窓には形状や開き方の種類が多数ありますが、同様に最近では環境負荷低減などを考慮したものも多数あります。デザインだけでなく、その機能も説明することが求められます。

examples

- ► The upper part of the window opens for ventilation.
  窓の上部は換気のために開きます。

- ► The window opens inwards for easier maintenance.
  窓はメンテナンスがより簡単な内開きとしました。

- ► A paired glass window is installed for severe climate conditions on site.
  敷地の厳しい気象条件を考慮し、ペアガラスが設置されています。

- ► A sun-shielding sheet is installed within paired glass to cope with sunlight from the west.
  西日対策として、ペアガラスの間に直射日光遮蔽シートを使用しています。

- ► The sliding doors have mesh glazing to prevent crime.
  引き戸には犯罪を防ぐためにメッシュガラスを採用しました。

Quick Chat | 咄嗟のひとこと

- Q: The window frame design is dull.
  窓枠デザインが野暮ったいな。

key phrases

open inwards
内に開く。反対語として open outwards 外に開く。
Strong winds should be considered when designing windows that open outwards.
外に向けて開く窓をデザインする時は強風を配慮しなければならない。

for maintenance
メンテナンスに配慮して

paired glass window
ペアガラス窓。laminated glass 合わせガラス。

for severe climate
厳しい天候に対して。厳しさには crucial や heavy や hard などがある。

sun-shielding sheet
日光遮蔽シート。関連表現に protect against UV rays 紫外線を防ぐ。遮るには shield や protect や block などの表現がある。

cope with〜
〜に対処する。同様の表現に deal with〜 がある。
The small windows are able to cope with hard winters.
小さな窓は厳しい冬に対応可能である。

to prevent crime
犯罪を防ぐために。防犯のために。
似た表現に for security がある。
Every window has a double-locking system for security.
全ての窓が防犯のために二重錠を付けている。

fixed windows
はめ殺し窓

sliding windows
引違い窓

pivot windows
回転窓

casement windows
開き窓

swing windows
突き出し窓

hopper windows
内倒し窓

single(double) hung windows
上げ下げ窓

louver windows
ルーバー窓

窓の種類

vocabulary

upper	上部の	mesh glazing	網目ガラス
ventilation	換気	bay windows	出窓
paired glass	ペアガラス	skylight	天窓
shielding	遮蔽した	shutter	雨戸
cope	対処する	sash	サッシ

 Shall we start researching a frameless window?
フレームレス窓を調べましょうか。

空間表現① (スケール・サイズ)
Scale/Size

スケールやサイズについて、単位を明確にしないと英訳したときに混乱します。例えば日本語で"高い"には、高低、温度、値段などを表現できますが英語ではそれぞれ違う表現になるので注意が必要です。

examples

▶ The unit-kitchen proposal is suitable for a limited budget and schedule.
キッチンユニット案は限られた予算と工期に相応しい。

▶ By adopting a basement and maintaining the gross area, the building is kept lower.
延べ床面積を維持し、地下を採用することで建物の高さを抑えます。

▶ The additional slope on the existing steps might be steeper than expected.
既存の段差に設置した斜路は想定より急になるかもしれません。

▶ The height of the shelves should be aligned with the others within 3mm.
棚の高さは他の棚と 3mm 以内の誤差で揃えてください。

▶ The thickness of the wall doesn't have as much presence as it does in the drawings.
壁の厚さは図面で見るほど存在感はありません。

▶ The single room with depth is divided into two rooms with sliding doors.
奥行きのあるワンルームは引き戸で分割できます。

Quick Chat | 咄嗟のひとこと

Q Is this height correct?
この高さで合っていますか？

key phrases

limited budget and schedule
限られた予算と工期

keep ~ low
～を低く抑える。keep~ はある状態を確保する。
Keep the entrance open.
玄関は開けておいて。

than expected
予想以上に。bigger (smaller) than expected 期待していたよりも大きかった（小さかった）。expect の他に anticipate や forecast などがある。

be aligned with~
～に揃えた

have presence
存在感がある

not much A than B
B ほど A ではない
The actual brightness of the color is not much weaker than that seen on the computer screen.
実際の色の明るさはコンピューターの画面で見るより弱くない。

with depth
奥行きのある

vocabulary

unit-kitchen	ユニットキッチン	step	階段
limited	限られた	steep	急な
budget	予算	height	高さ
basement	地下階	thickness	厚さ
additional	加えられた、追加の	presence	存在感
slope	斜路、スロープ	depth	奥行き
existing	現存する、既存の	oppressive	圧迫感がある

 It's right, but does it feel oppressive?
正しいです。しかし圧迫感が出てきますか。

空間表現② (閉じる・開く)
Close/Open

「地域に開く」、「内に開く」など日本特有の空間表現には英語で表現しづらいものが多くがあります。その曖昧な境界の話は日本人特有の距離感の元に成立していることを理解したうえで説明する必要があります。

examples

- A part of the garden is also open to the neighboring community.
  この庭の一部は近隣コミュニティーにも開いています。

- The house is close to the neighbors. Therefore, the external envelope has small openings.
  この住宅は近隣と距離が近い。そのため外壁には小さな開口部を設けました。

- While having a narrow entrance on the side opening to the road, the residence has wide openings on the side facing the coast.
  住宅には道路側に開かれた小さな玄関がある一方で、沿岸側には広い間口が設けられている。

- The laboratories have glass partitions to allow for visual connections.
  研究室群は視覚上のつながりを得るためガラスの仕切りとしました。

- Eye-level partitions mean that every worker senses their colleagues in the next booth.
  目線の高さのパーティションによって全ての職員は隣の同僚の気配を感じます。

💡 Quick Chat | 咄嗟のひとこと

- **Q:** We should think about the character of the corner site.
  角地の特性を考えるべきです。

key phrases

open to~
~に対して開けている
The ground floor of the library should be a space open to the public.
図書館の地上階は市民に開放されるべきだ。

close to~
~に近い。close は閉じる〔動詞〕だけでなく、近い〔形容詞〕もある。
The house is built close to the cliff edge.
その家は崖の淵の近くに建設されている。

external envelope
外壁。envelope〔名詞〕封筒の他に、外皮、膜という意味もある。

while~
~の一方で。似た表現で meanwhile がある。
The entrance opening is quite simple. Meanwhile, the internal space is complex.
玄関開口部は非常にシンプルです。一方で内部空間は複雑です。

for visual connection
視覚上のつながりのために
There is a visual connection between the private area and the public space.
プライベートエリアからパブリックスペースに向けて視覚上のつながりがあります。

eye-level
目線の高さの
Visitors cannot see the inside of the meeting room due to the eye-level frosted glass partition.
訪問者は目線の高さにある曇りガラスのパーティションによって会議室の中を見ることができません。

---

vocabulary

neighboring community　近隣のコミュニティー、近隣のつながり	visual　視覚上の
	connection　つながり
external envelope　外壁	sense　（気配を）感じる
opening　開口部	booth　ブース、ボックス席、仕切り席
wide　広い	cliff edge　崖の淵
partition　区切り	complex　複雑な

 Why don't we open the front garden to the neighbors?
前庭を近隣に開放してはどうでしょう。

31 空間表現③（曖昧な表現）
Ambiguous Expression

日本人には曖昧なものを好む傾向があります。建築空間においては完全に閉じたり、開いたりしないなど、その緩やかなつながりを表現するには多少説明的になる必要があります。

examples

- The entrance hall has spaciousness due to an ambiguous partition.
  玄関ホールは曖昧な仕切りによって空間の広がりがあります。

- The office floor has a sense of being one space because of the eye-level height of partitions.
  オフィスフロアは目線高さのパーティションによって空間の一体感があります。

- The garden view at the entrance hall welcomes the guests.
  玄関ホールの庭の景色が訪問者を迎えます。

- The area boundary is clarified by lights in a recess on the ceiling.
  領域の境界は天井の折り上げ照明によって明確にします。

- The entrance corridor with wooden walls gives a warm feeling to visitors.
  木製の壁による玄関廊下は訪問者に温かな気持ちを提供します。

- The display panel is made to stand out by being lifted from the wall.
  展示パネルは壁から浮き上がらせることで際立ちます。

🎙 Quick Chat ｜咄嗟のひとこと

Q Can we introduce an *engawa* facing the garden?
　庭に面した縁側を作りましょうか？

key phrases

ambiguous partition
曖昧な仕切り。ambiguous に似た表現は ambivalent、obscure、opaque、unclear、vague など。
We will use an opaque glazing partition wall to surround the consulting space.
私たちはコンサルティング室の周囲に不透明なガラスを使いましょう。

sense of being one space
空間の一体感

clarify
明確にする
The partition wall clarifies the space used by visitors.
仕切り壁は訪問者が使う場所を明確にする。

lights in a recess on the ceiling
折り上げ照明。recess 奥まった場所、recessed wall くぼんだ場所のある壁。

give a warm feeling
暖かみを与える

stand out
目立つ。似た表現に highlight 際立たせる、emphasize 強調する。
The panels are emphasized by colored edges.
パネルは色付けされた縁で目立たせている。

lift from～
～から持ち上げる
When guests come into this room, the bed is lifted from the floor.
訪問者がこの部屋に入ったとき、ベッドは床から持ち上げられる。

---

vocabulary

spaciousness 広大さ	corridor 廊下
ambiguous 曖昧な	wooden 木造の
welcome 迎える	lifted 浮き上がった、持ち上がった
clarify 明確にする	emphasize 強調する
recess 奥まった場所	gentle connection 緩やかなつながり
ceiling 天井	

Step 1 | Conveying Design Ideas | デザインの魅力を伝える

 It would be a good idea to create gentle connections to the rooms.
部屋との緩やかなつながりが生まれて良い考えですね。

32 空間表現④ (程度)
Grade

日本人は自身の気持ちや考えを他人に表現するのが苦手です。それゆえ自分の提案の良さや特徴を相手に伝えるのならば多少誇張した表現で丁度良いのかも知れません。

examples

- Luxurious materials have been used for the reception area.
  受付周辺は豪華な建材を使いました。

- The site is thoroughly covered with thick snow in winter season.
  敷地は冬になると深い雪に一面覆われます。

- The site is surrounded by beautiful, untouched nature.
  敷地は美しい手付かずの自然環境に囲まれています。

- The building site that was previously in a poor condition will become a communal area.
  以前劣悪な環境だった建物の敷地は市民の憩いの場となるでしょう。

- Once this museum opens, the number of tourists in this city will rocket.
  この博物館が開館するれば、この街への観光客数は激増するでしょう。

- The building facade has been made as simple and modest as possible.
  この建築のファサードは極力シンプルかつ控えめにしました。

Quick Chat | 咄嗟のひとこと

What a beautiful view this is!
なんと素晴らしい景色でしょう！

key phrases

thoroughly covered with~
～で一面覆われる。thoroughly すっかり、完全に。thoroughly wet びっしょり濡れる。

be surrounded by~
～で囲まれた。似た意味で enclosed がある。
The building is surrounded by many other skyscraper buildings.
そのビルは他の多くの高層ビルに囲われている。

in a poor condition
劣悪な環境にある

once~
一度～すれば、一度の
The facility needs to be checked once a month.
この施設は月に一度、点検する必要がある。
The Olympic Games are a once-in-a-lifetime event.
五輪は一生に一度のイベントである。

rocket
急上昇する。急騰する。数値などが飛び上がる際に表現される。似た表現に increase dramatically。

as ~ as possible
可能な限り～、極力～。用例としては as soon as possible なるべく早く、がある。その略語である ASAP はメールなどの文章でよく使われる。

vocabulary

luxurious	高級感のある	previously	以前に
reception	受付	poor	劣悪な、貧相な
thoroughly	完全に	condition	状況
covered	覆われた	communal	共同の
thick	厚い、深みのある	once	一度
surrounded	囲まれた	rocket	跳ね上がる
untouched nature	手つかずの自然	modest	控えめな、謙遜している

 The site location is everything in this project.
この敷地がこのプロジェクトの全てだ。

33 色（濃淡・明度・彩度）
Color/Shading/Brightness/Chroma

建築を構成する需要な要素に「色」があります。しかし、色を説明するには明暗や濃淡など様々な要素とともに、時に「詩的」に表現する必要があります。

examples

- The building wall was colored green to match the natural environment.
  建物壁面は周辺環境に調和させるために緑色とした。

- The gallery space is painted with pale colors.
  展示スペースは淡い色使いで塗られています。

- The dark and tranquil internal space is disconnected from the disturbing urban hustle and bustle.
  暗く落ち着いた内部空間は都市の喧噪から隔離されている。

- We described the place of prayer as a "dense space".
  私たちは祈りの空間を"濃度のある空間"と表現しました。

- Whilst white color reflects light, black absorbs it.
  白色は光を反射する一方で、黒色は光を吸収する。

 Quick Chat ｜ 咄嗟のひとこと

 Is this color too dark?
この色は暗すぎませんか？

key phrases

match
調和する。match〔名詞〕試合、競争相手。be a match for~/ ~に匹敵する、~に似つかわしい。

disconnect A from B
BからAを隔離する

describe A as B
AをBと表現する。description〔名詞〕表現。

dense space
濃度のある空間。関連表現に airy space 軽快な空間など。

whilst~
~の一方で。同じ意味で while もある。

reflect light/absorb light
光を反射する／光を吸収する

---

vocabulary

color 色、着色する	hustle and bustle 喧騒
match 調和する	describe 描く、表現する
pale 薄い（色彩的に）	prayer 祈り
tranquil 落ち着いた	dense 濃厚な
internal 内部空間	reflect 反射する
disconnected 隔離された	absorb 吸収する
disturbing 煩い、邪魔な	

 No, we need tranquility in this room.
いや、この部屋には落ち着きが必要なのです。

テクスチャー
Texture

触覚や視覚を表現するには、適切な単語を活用するのも大切ですが、その背景情報も一緒に表現することで伝わりやすくなります。

examples

- This shiny material is beautiful, but it isn't suitable for the external wall.
  このきらっと光る素材は美しいが、外装には向かない。

- All furniture in the kindergarten has to be tough enough for use by children.
  幼稚園内の全ての家具は子供たちの使用に耐えうるように頑丈でなければならない。

- Which is better, the clay wall with the rough surface, or the plaster wall with the smooth surface?
  ざらついた土壁の触感と、磨かれたしっくいの触感、どちらが良いだろう？

- The door should be rigid and robust enough to endure repeated use.
  ドアは繰り返しの使用に耐えらえれる丈夫で頑丈な作りにしなければならない。

- Solid pieces are applied to express the massiveness of the material.
  量塊な部材が素材の重厚感を出すために活用される。

- Stretchy material has been adopted for the installation in the tradeshow.
  伸縮性のある建材が展示会のインスタレーションに採用されました。

Quick Chat | 咄嗟のひとこと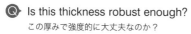

- Is this thickness robust enough?
  この厚みで強度的に大丈夫なのか？

key phrases

tough enough
　十分に頑丈な。tough に似た表現で firm、robust、solid、strong、substantial など。

which is better, A or B?
　AとBどちらが良いですか？

endure repeated use
　繰り返しの使用に耐える

---

vocabulary

shiny　ツヤのある、光っている	repeated use　繰り返しの使用
kindergarten　幼稚園	solid　塊の
tough　しっかりした、硬い	massiveness　重厚感
rough　粗い	stretchy　伸縮性のある
smooth　なめらかな	installation　インスタレーション、展示物（作品）
robust　頑丈な	
endure　耐える	

 At three millimeters, it should be fine.
　3mmですが、十分かと。

明るさ・照明
Brightness/Lighting

明るさの感覚は日本人と海外の人では大きく異なることがあります。照明器具の詳細な説明も大切ですがその見え方の違いを理解したうえで明るさを表現しましょう。

examples

- The interior space requires an adequate lighting plan.
  内部空間は適切な照明計画が求められます。

- The pendant lightings would be suitable for the tables.
  ペンダントライトがテーブル席に相応しいかも知れません。

- The reflection from the building on the opposite side of the road is extremely bright.
  通りの向かいのビルの反射が非常にまぶしい。

- Would you please submit the reflected lighting ceiling plan as soon as possible?
  照明天井伏図の提出を早急にお願いできますか？

- The bicycle parking space has sensor-controlled lighting for nighttime use.
  夜間使用のために、駐輪場はセンサー付き照明としました。

Quick Chat ｜咄嗟のひとこと

It's a good idea to choose indirect lighting.
間接照明を選んだのは良い考えだ。

key phrases

pendant lighting
ペンダント（吊り下げ型）ライト。suspend 吊るす。
The air conditioning duct is suspended from a concrete soffit.
空調ダクトはコンクリートスラブから吊り下げられている。

would be〜
〜だろう。意見を述べる際の丁寧な表現でとてもよく使われる。

be suitable for〜
〜に相応しい
A long-life LED light is suitable for the high ceiling space.
長寿命の LED 照明は高天井に相応しい。

on the opposite side of the road
道路の反対側。似た表現に on the other side of the road。道路の同じ側では on the same side of the road.

reflected lighting ceiling plan
照明天井伏図。天井伏図は reflected ceiling plan とする。
Some newcomer architects don't understand the concept of a reflected ceiling plan.
新人の建築士は天井照明伏図の考えを理解できない。

間接照明の納まり例

vocabulary

require　必要とする
adequate　十分な
pendant　ペンダントの、吊り下げられた
suitable　適切な
reflection　反射
opposite　反対の

extremely　極端な
bright　まぶしい、明るい
submit　提出する
possible　可能である
sensor-controlled　センサー付きの
nighttime use　夜間使用

A This option allows lighting to be hidden and avoids reflection on the ceiling.　こうすることで、光源を隠して、映り込みも避けることができています。

36 透明度
Transparency

透明度はガラスの透過率の話もありますが、曖昧な境界や見え方を説明するために使われる表現でもあります。

examples

- The large opening uses opaque glass to prevent viewing from the street.
  通りからの視線をさえぎるために大きな開口部には不透明ガラスを使います。

- The perforated panels are cladded to act as a translucent screen.
  有孔板は透過スクリーンとして外装材に使用されます。

- Paired glass in which Japanese paper is inserted demonstrates a unique opacity.
  和紙を挟んだペアガラスは独特な不透明さを演出します。

- Do you know any local factories that provide high-transparency glass?
  透明度の高いガラスを提供する現地の工場をご存知ですか？

- A special pattern has been printed on the glass surface with the expectation that it will have a moire effect.
  モアレ効果を期待して特別なパターンがガラス面に印刷された。

- This glass looks slightly greener.
  このガラスはちょっと緑っぽく見えます。

Quick Chat | 咄嗟のひとこと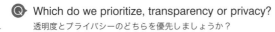

Q: Which do we prioritize, transparency or privacy?
透明度とプライバシーのどちらを優先しましょうか？

key phrases

prevent~ing
～するのを妨げる、～するのを防ぐ。似た意味に protect や disturb や prohibit。
The hedge protects against viewing from outside.
生け垣は外からの視線を防ぎます。

be cladded
（外装材として）覆われた、外装材とする。cladding〔名詞〕外装材、clad〔動詞〕覆う。

with the expectation that~
～と期待して

slightly
少し、多少。似たような表現では a little などがある。
The transparency of this window is a little weaker.
この窓の透明度はちょっと弱いです。

---

vocabulary

opaque 不透明な	provide 提供する
prevent 防ぐ	transparency 透明度
perforated 多孔質の	pattern パターン、模様
clad 覆う	surface 表面
translucent 半透明の	expectation 期待
demonstrate 演出する	moire effect モアレ効果
opacity 不透明性	since~ ～なので

 Since it is the office floor, it should be transparency.
オフィスですから、透明度でしょう。

37 インテリア① (各地のスタイル)
Interior (local styles)

海外の文化を参照する際、すぐにその本質を理解するのは困難です。同様に日本のデザインを海外に伝えるときも、多少誇張する（ベタにする）ぐらいで丁度良いと思います。

examples

- ▶ The restaurant has been designed with an Asian atmosphere to match the food menu.
  レストランは提供されるメニューに合わせてアジア風のインテリアとしました。

- ▶ The simple Japanese design stands out against the brickwork.
  日本のシンプルなデザインがレンガ造に際立ちます。

- ▶ Project staff working on projects in the Middle East should learn about religious manners.
  中東のプロジェクトに関わっているスタッフは宗教マナーについて学ばなければならない。

- ▶ In Europe, people sometimes like bath tubs with claw feet.
  欧州では時々猫足のバスタブが好まれます。

- ▶ Interiors with half-Japanese and half-Western designs are suitable for contemporary life.
  和洋折衷のインテリアが現代の生活に似合うようです。

Quick Chat | 咄嗟のひとこと

Q: Is this Japanese style?
これが和風なのですか？

key phrases

stand out against~
〜に対して際立つ

work on~
〜を担当する、〜に取り組む

religious manner
宗教上のマナー
We shouldn't talk about religion in the office.
私たちはオフィスの中で宗教の話をするべきではない。

suit~
〜に対して相応しい、〜に似合う。suitable 適切な。
Modern buildings are sometimes ill-suited to rural districts.
近代的な建物は田舎地方では時々似合わない。

Japanese style
和風。日本人が「欧米人」と一括りにするように、日本のデザインをアジアデザインと把握されることがあるので説明しなければなりません。
Japanese style design expresses simplicity such as that of Zen philosophy.
和風デザインは禅哲学のシンプルさを表現している。

---

vocabulary

atmosphere　雰囲気
match　合う
brickwork　レンガ造
religious　宗教上の
manner　マナー、風習、作法

claw feet　猫足の
harf-Japanese and harf-Western
　和洋折衷の
comtemporary life　現代の生活

 Yes, this is recognized as Japanese style overseas.
はい、これが海外で理解されている和風です。

インテリア② (本物・偽物)
Interior (Authentic/Fake)

デザイン要素や考え方で参照したもの、特にそれが日本オリジナルのものならば、言葉はもちろんのこと、写真や図版などできちんと説明したいものです。また、必ずしも本物でなくとも代用品をうまく使う提案は V.E (Value Engineering) としても評価されやすいでしょう。

examples

- Fake materials shouldn't be used under eye level.
  偽物の素材は目線の高さ以下に使うべきではない。

- To be honest, we should insist on using genuine products for the retail interior materials.
  正直なところ、店舗内装の建材は本物を使うことにこだわるべきです。

- Although we love using genuine brickwork, in this case we will go for the alternative choice of tiles.
  本物のレンガを使いたいところだが、今回は代用品としてタイルにしておきましょう。

- We should use authentic materials to express contrast with the existing building.
  既存建物への対比を演出するには、本物の素材を使用すべきです。

- Materials can't change the essence of space.
  素材は空間の本質を変えられません。

- This design does not mimic but makes reference to other designs.
  このデザインは他のデザインを真似しているのではなく、参照しているのです。

💡 Quick Chat | 咄嗟のひとこと

Q: Won't people soon lose interest if we use trend design?
もし流行のデザインを使用すれば、すぐに飽きられませんか？

key phrases

to be honest
正直に言うと。To be honest with you でより丁寧な意味合いになる。

use for~
~に使用する
Durable materials should be used for the external wall.
丈夫な建材が外壁で使われるべきです。

insist on~
~にこだわる
The architects insist on genuine materials.
建築家は本物の材料にこだわる。

contrast with~
~との対比

make reference to~
~を参照する、参考にする

lose interest
飽きる

---

vocabulary

fake 偽物の	mimic 真似をする
insist こだわる、固執する	durable 丈夫な
genuine 本物の	trend 流行の
authentic 本物の	standard 定番の、標準的な
contrast 対比	

 It is standard now rather than a trend.
それは流行というよりも今や定番のデザインです。

家具とその配置
Furniture and Layout

家具はその素材、詳細、そして使われ方などを説明します。また備え付けの造作家具のように間取りや空間に影響を及ぼす場合、建築的に説明する必要があります。

examples

- The furniture layout has been designed with consideration for the blind.
  家具の配置については、目の見えない人へ配慮して計画しました。

- The bathroom has handrails so that it can be continually used by senior residents.
  高齢居住者の継続的な利用のために、浴室には手すりがあります。

- Stacking chairs are recommended for the meeting rooms.
  積み上げ式椅子が会議室にはお勧めです。

- The table and chair layout should be considered to promote lively discussion among the participants.
  机とテーブルの配置は参加者たちの活発な議論のために考えなければならない。

- The bookshelves have been arranged so that users feel as if they are walking through an information forest.
  利用者が情報の森の中を歩いているように本棚を配置した。

- The corners of furniture are rounded off because many children will use them.
  多くの幼児が使うので、家具の角を丸くしています。

Quick Chat ｜咄嗟のひとこと

Q: Has the client requested their own furniture?
施主要望の家具はあるのか？

key phrases

furniture layout
家具の配置。配置には position、allocation、location、arrangement、placement などがある。
When you think about the room interior, you should do some research into furniture layout.
部屋の内装を考えるときには、家具の配置場所についても検討すべきである。

the blind
目の見えない人＝ blind people。the ＋形容詞で人を意味する。例：the deaf 聴覚障がい者、the young 若者、the old 高齢者。

stacking chairs
積み上げ椅子。stackable chair ともいう。folding chair 折り畳み式椅子。

as if~
まるで～のように

rounded off
丸められた。類似表現に trimmed off 切り取る。

---

vocabulary

consideration　配慮	stacking　積み上げ式の
blind　盲目の	recommend　お勧めする
handrail　手すり	promote　促す
continually　継続して	lively　活発な
senior resident　高齢者の住人	fixed shelf　造り付けの棚

Ⓐ　Yes, he has requested three fixed shelves.
　　はい、造り付けの棚 3 つを希望していました。

仕上げ① (外装)
Cladding Exterior

外装材は躯体との関係性、建材の説明はもちろんのこと、磨き方やはつり方など仕上げ表現もきちんと説明したいところです。

examples

- ▶ Traditional brickwork has been applied to preserve the townscape.
  街並みを維持するため伝統的なレンガ造を採用しました。

- ▶ The balustrade on the roof terrace is made of metal for maintenance.
  屋上テラスの欄干は維持管理のために鉄製です。

- ▶ Galvalume steel plates are an affordable material. Moreover, they create expressive wall surfaces.
  ガルバリウム鋼板は安価な材料です。そのうえ、表情豊かな壁面を作れます。

- ▶ Glazing panels are installed on the facade of the main street and ALC paneling on the rest of the facades to reduce the cost.
  通りに面したファサードはガラス張りにして、それ以外はコストを抑えるためにALCパネルです。

- ▶ Scratch-proof hardboard timber has been adopted for the skirting.
  傷に強い木材が巾木に採用されました。

- ▶ The floor tile surface is grooved for drainage and slip resistance.
  床タイル表面は排水と滑り防止のために溝を付けました。

💬 Quick Chat | 咄嗟のひとこと

Q. The building has an exposed concrete finish.
建物はコンクリートの打ち放しの仕上げにしよう。

key phrases

for maintenance
維持管理のために
The external wall needs to be washable for maintenance.
外壁は維持管理のために洗浄可能の必要がある。

be grooved
溝の付いた。groove〔名詞〕溝、〔動詞〕溝をつける。他に溝には slot や gutter や trench などがある。

slip resistance
滑り止め。類語は slip-proof。
Slip-proof tape is applied at the stair nose.
滑り止めテープが段鼻に貼られる。

scratch-proof
傷のつきにくい、傷防止の。似た表現で scratch resistance。
The protective film on the glass is scratch-resistant.
ガラスに貼られた保護フィルムは傷つき防止です。

---

vocabulary

preserve　維持する	smooth finish　繊細な仕上げ
balustrade　手すり、欄干	autoclaved lightweight concrete panel　ALC パネル
galvalume steel plate　ガルバリウム鋼板	sprayed material　吹き付け材
skirting　幅木	siding(external finishing wall)　サイディング（外壁に貼る仕上げ板材）
exposed concrete　打ち放しコンクリート	roof tile　瓦
rough finish　粗い仕上げ	slate　スレート

 Will it have a rough finish, or smooth one?
荒々しい仕上げですか？　なめらかにしますか？

仕上げ② (内装)
Interior

内装仕上げ処理については、日本の建材メーカーのカタカナ名称がそのままでは伝わらないことがあります。その場合は目的を伝えながら説明すると伝わりやすくなります。

examples

- The reception desk counter has a clear-lacquered finish to give it a luxurious feel.
  受付デスクの天板は高級感を出すためにクリアラッカー仕上げとしています。

- The interior design uses traditional decoration to show local culture.
  内装デザインは地元文化を見せるために伝統的な装飾を使います。

- The concrete floor has a hammered finish to provide slip resistance in rainy conditions.
  コンクリート床は雨天時のスリップ防止のために斫り仕上げとしました。

- The steel claddings are finished with sandblast to make them fingerprint-proof.
  鉄製外装材は指紋が付かないように砂吹き(サンドブラスト)仕上げとします。

- Do you know the difference between soft and hard water in relation to the local plaster?
  現地の漆喰に対する軟水や硬水の違いについてご存知ですか？

Quick Chat | 咄嗟のひとこと

Is the construction method difficult?
施工方法は難しいですか？

key phrases

clear-lacquered finish
クリアラッカー仕上げの。ペンキの仕上げには matte finish、satin finish、eggshell finish ともに艶消し、gloss finish 艶仕上げ、などがある。

give a luxurious feel
高級感を出す。仕上げには hammered finish 斫り仕上げの、sandblasted 砂吹き、polished、honed ともに磨き、brushed ブラシ磨き、などがある。

rainy conditions
雨天時の。天候の表現には、thunderstorm conditions 雷の嵐の中、strong wind conditions 強風の中、heatwave conditions 熱波の中、deep snow conditions 深い雪で、hail conditions ヒョウが降る中、などがある。

fingerprint-proof
指紋防止。
The mirrored finish door is sealed with fingerprint-resistant film.
鏡面仕上げのドアは指紋防止フィルムが貼られている。

in relation to〜
〜に対する、〜に関する

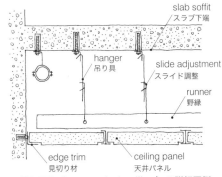

吊り天井（suspended ceiling）の詳細図例

vocabulary

- clear-lacquered クリアラッカーの
- hammer ハンマーで打ち付ける
- slip resistance 滑り止め
- cladding 外装材
- sandblast 砂吹き、サンドブラスト
- fingerprint 指紋
- soft/hard water 軟水、硬水
- plaster 漆喰
- solid wood flooring 無垢材フローリング
- vinyl sheet (tile) flooring クッション床
- linoleum flooring リノリウム床
- cork flooring コルク床
- tatami mat 畳
- wall paper クロス（壁紙）
- painted wall 塗り壁
- fiber reinforced plastic(FRP) FRP樹脂
- terrazzo 人造大理石

 No, we have special experience of doing that.
いえ、私たちには特別の経験があります。

42 アクティビティ
Activity

「佇む」、「溜る」など人間の行動に沿った機能空間を想定するのならば、まずはその可視化しづらい現象を明確に説明しなければなりません。

examples

- The rest spaces for elderly people are located at the street corners of the community.
  老人の佇める場所を地域の街角に計画しています。

- The steps have a function as spaces where people can gather.
  階段は人が溜る場としても機能します。

- There are enclosed workspaces to aid concentration of users.
  利用者が集中するための閉じた執務空間があります。

- The company expects new inspiration to emerge out of discussions among its co-workers.
  会社は同僚との議論で新しい発想が生まれることを期待します。

- Do we have a way of making people's activity in the buildings visible without using a glass facade?
  ガラス張りファサードを使わずに内部を可視化する方法はないでしょうか？

- A screen with Japanese paper and opaque glazing might mean that the appearance of the interior filters outside the room.
  和紙や不透明ガラスのスクリーンは室内の様子が外へ染み出すように見えるかもしれません。

- Many different types of spaces are planned in the large floor so that workers can also relax alone.
  様々な種類の居場所を大きなフロアに設けることで、一人でもくつろげる場所となります。

Quick Chat | 咄嗟のひとこと

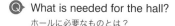 What is needed for the hall?
ホールに必要なものとは？

key phrases

street corner
街角。関連語に block 区画、community 地域社会、district 区域。

aid concentration
集中を促す。concentrate 集中する。類似語に focus 集中する。

emerge out of discussion
議論から生まれる

discussion among~
〜同士での議論、〜間の議論
We need a discussion among all team leaders on site at once.
今すぐ現場の全チームリーダーによる議論が必要です。

vocabulary

rest 休憩する、たたずむ	concentrate 集中する
elderly 高齢の	emerge 発生する
gather 集う、溜まる	co-worker 同僚
enclosed 閉じた	filter 染み出す

 It should be a space where visitors can gather.
訪問者が溜れる場所だろう。

日本特有の法規
Japanese Construction Law

日本の「建築基準法」の英語対訳が必ず存在するとは限りません。それゆえ、英語表現が多少説明的になってもやむを得ないと思います。

examples

- The volume layout for this site exceeds the shadow restrictions.
  この敷地のボリューム配置は日影規制に引っかかります。

- We can't increase the volume due to the floor area ratio of this site.
  この敷地の容積率の制限から、これ以上の容積を取れません。

- There is a building height restriction, defined by the width of the front road.
  敷地に面している道路幅から規定される建物の高さ制限があります。

- This area is defined as a commercial district.
  このエリアは商業地域と決められています。

- A public meeting for local residents is required to approve this plan.
  地元の住民説明会がこの計画を承認するために必要です。

Quick Chat | 咄嗟のひとこと

Q: First of all, we should check the regulations on this site.
まず最初に、この敷地にはどのような規制があるのか調べるべきです。

key phrases

due to~
～によって、～に従って

floor area ratio
容積率。関連語に site area 敷地面積、building area 建築面積、floor area 床面積、total floor area 延べ面積。

height restriction
道路高さ制限（前面道路との関係からの高さ制限。通称：道路斜線）、height restriction defined by the distance from the site boundaries 隣地高さ制限（隣地境界との関係からの高さ制限。通称：隣地斜線）、height restriction defined by the distance from the north site boundary 北側高さ制限（北側境界との関係からの高さ制限。通称：北側斜線）

be defined by~
～によって規定される、～によって決められる。関連語に defined as~/～と定められる

commercial district
商業地域。用途地域の一般名称としては他に residential district 住宅地域、industrial district 工業地域などがある。

vocabulary

volume　ボリューム、塊	public meeting　住民説明会
exceed　超過する、上回る	resident　住人
shadow restriction　日影規制	require　必要とする
ratio　率、割合	approve　承認する
height restriction　高さ制限	open space ratio　空地率
define　定義する	comprehensive design system　総合設計制度
width　幅	public open space　公開空地
front road　前面道路	building coverage ratio　建蔽率
commercial　商業の	

A OK. I will do A. S. A. P.
了解です。なるべく早く調べます。

44 法規
Construction Law

建築法規はその国によって独自の解釈があります。誤解を防ぐためにも、十分にその国（日本も含めた）の法規を理解し、説明する必要があります。

examples

- The height of the building has been lowered to comply with the height limit for this district.
  建物の高さはこの地域の高さ制限に従って低く抑えられた。

- We have to investigate whether the escape route is adequate or not.
  避難経路が適切かどうか検討しなければならない。

- How much time does it normally take to approve planning permission?
  建築許可が承認されるまでに通常どれぐらいの時間がかかりますか？

- Is it possible for a local collaborator to apply for planning permission?
  建築許可は現地の協働者によって申請することは可能ですか？

- In Japan, the slope is defined by the gradient regulation. How about in your country?
  日本ではスロープは勾配規制によって決められています。現地ではどうですか？

Quick Chat | 咄嗟のひとこと

Q. What is the gradient of this ramp?
　　この斜路の角度は？

key phrases

lower
低くする。low（低い：形容詞）の動詞。関連語に widen 広げる（wide の動詞形）。
The path was widened to 4m.
その小道は 4m 幅に広げられた。

comply with~
~に従って、~に合わせて

investigate
調査する、検討する
Would you investigate the height restriction law in your country?
あなたの国の高さ規制の法律を調査していただけますか？

how much time does it take to~
~するのにどのくらい時間がかかりますか？

by the gradient regulation
勾配規制によって

How about~?
~はどうですか？ 例文や以下の文のように、前半の文章を受けて How about~? と使用する。
We haven't had a pay rise in recent years. How about in your company?
弊社は近年昇給がありません。御社はどうですか？

---

vocabulary

height 高さ	normally 通常は
lower 低くする	approve 承認する
height limit 高さ制限	planning permission 建築許可
district 地域	collaborator 協働者
investigate 調査する	slope/ramp 斜路、スロープ
escape route 避難経路	gradient 勾配
adequate 適切な	

 It is one eight.
1/8 です。

構造
Structure

設計者は構造について、概念として理解し、図示できることも信頼を得るためには必要です。

examples

- ► This column cannot be omitted from the perspective of earthquake resistance.
  耐震性の観点からこの柱は省略することができない。

- ► The old building is being refurbished with a quake-absorbing structure instead of being demolished.
  古い建築は壊す代わりに免震構造で改修している。

- ► The beam holding the roof slab is made from pre-stressed concrete.
  屋根スラブを支える梁はプレストレストコンクリートでできている。

- ► The beam section has compression on the top half and tension on the bottom.
  梁断面には上部で圧縮、下部で引っ張りの力がかかっている。

- ► The height of the beam will be taller to realize the long span of the space.
  この空間の大スパンを実現するために梁せいは高くなるでしょう。

- ► The column size and numbers can be researched using several different options.
  柱のサイズと数は、いくつか異なるパターンを使って検討できます。

Quick Chat | 咄嗟のひとこと

Q: Shall we thicken the columns?
　　柱を太くしましょうか？

key phrases

from the perspective of~
　〜の観点から

be refurbished with~
　〜で改修される。refurbish の類語に renovate 改修する。

quake-absorbing structure
　免震構造。関連語に earthquake-proof structure、earthquake-resistant structure ともに耐震構造、shake-proof 耐震の、など。

beam
　梁。他の構造部材として floor 床、column 柱、brace 筋交い、structural wall 構造壁。truss トラス。

vocabulary

column　柱
omit　省く、外す
earthquake resistance　耐震性
quake-absorbing structure　免震構造
demolish　取り壊す
beam　梁
hold　支える
slab　スラブ、厚板

pre-stressed concrete　プレストレストコンクリート
section　断面
compression　圧縮
tension　引っ張り
height of the beam　梁せい
thicken　太くする
brace　筋交い

 No, we should add braces.
　いや、筋交いを入れるべきです。

構法
Construction Method

日本の伝統工法などを英語で表現する際、一般的な単語の対訳がない場合があります。その際には図版や写真とともに周辺状況なども丁寧に説明すると良いでしょう。

> **examples**
>
> ▶ The building has a timber structure that utilizes traditional Japanese construction methods.
> この建築物は日本の伝統的工法である木造を採用します。
>
> ▶ Prefabricated containers are proposed for victims in the devastated area.
> プレファブユニット型コンテナが災害地の被災者に提案されます。
>
> ▶ The brick wall surface is tied to the reinforced concrete structure inside.
> レンガ壁の外観は内側の鉄筋コンクリート構造体に留められています。
>
> ▶ Exposed concrete requires extra care in humid environments.
> コンクリート打ち放しは湿気環境に特別の配慮が求められる。
>
> ▶ It might be possible to erect the temporary structure with steel pipes if we don't worry about making it shakeproof.
> もし耐震性を気にしなくてよければ、鉄パイプでの仮設建築を建てるのは可能かもしれない。

🍄 *Quick Chat* ｜咄嗟のひとこと

 Can we use brickwork as a structure?
レンガは構造体として使えますか？

key phrases

timber structure

木造。同じ意味で wooden structure がある。steel structure 鉄骨構造、reinforced concrete structure 鉄筋コンクリート構造、steel-framed reinforced concrete structure 鉄骨鉄筋コンクリート構造。Cross Laminated Timber：CLT（直交集成板）。

prefabricated method

プレファブ工法。brickwork レンガ造、blockwork ブロック造、stone structure 石造り。
The machine room is enclosed by a brickwork wall.
機械室はレンガ造壁で囲われている。

be tied to~

～に留められる。関連語に be connected to~/ ～に繋げられる。
The blockwork wall is connected to the concrete wall at 6m intervals.
ブロック造壁はコンクリート壁に 6m 毎に繋げられている。

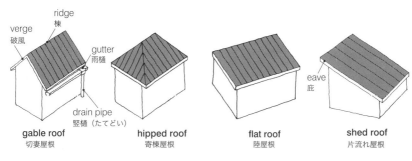

屋根の種類

vocabulary

timber 木の	steel-framed reinforced concrete structure 鉄骨鉄筋コンクリート造
construction method 構法	steel-framed structure 鉄骨造
reinforced concrete 鉄筋コンクリート	masonry structure 組積造
exposed concrete むき出しの、打ち放しコンクリート	frame structure ラーメン構造
extra care 特別の配慮	brace structure ブレース構造
humid 湿気のある	wall structure 壁構造
steel pipe 鉄パイプ	traditional construction method 在来工法
shakeproof 耐震の	dome structure ドーム構造
wooden(timber) structure 木造	shell structure シェル構造
reinforced concrete structure 鉄筋コンクリート造	

Ⓐ No, we can't in this country.
この国では不可能です。

47 設備
Services

設備系統は大体対訳となる英語があります。図示や正確な数値とともに説明することで相手に伝わります。

examples

- A ventilation tower with a 10m height is required to provide sufficient ventilation for spaces under the ground.
  地下空間の適切な換気のために高さ10mの換気塔が必要です。

- The gap between the structure and duct is filled with fire-rated foam.
  構造体とダクトの隙間は耐火フォームで塞ぎます。

- The blockwork wall has a conduit for electrical cable tubes connecting to the switch box.
  ブロック壁には電源ボックスへつながる配線チューブ用の溝があります。

- The water tank requires a concrete plinth beneath and maintenance space around.
  貯水タンクには下部にコンクリ土台と周囲に管理スペースが必要です。

- The raised floor needs to be at least 20cm high to give the drain pipes a sufficient flow angle.
  上げ床は十分な排水角度のパイプのために少なくとも20cmの高さが必要になる。

- Each fire extinguisher is required to cover a 20m radius on service floors.
  それぞれの消火器は設備階において半径20mをカバーするように要求される。

💡 Quick Chat ｜咄嗟のひとこと

Q When will we have a response from the mechanical engineer?
設備技師からの返事は何時来ますか？

key phrases

gap between A and B
A と B の隙間

conduit
溝。溝には groove、gutter、slot、trench などもある。
The machine room floor requires a gutter along the edge of the room.
機械室の床は室内の端に溝が求められています。

beneath
下に。似た表現では under、below。上に above、top など。周囲に around。

maintenance space
管理スペース
This room needs 0.6m of clearance around the water tank to allow for maintenance.
この部屋には貯水槽の周囲に管理のために 0.6m の空間が必要です。

flow angle
流れる角度。角度の程度を表すには steep、sharp 急な、gentle 緩やかなどがある。

---

vocabulary

ventilation tower　換気塔	plinth　土台
under the ground　地下に	beneath　下に
gap　隙間	around　周囲に
duct　ダクト、管	raised floor　上げ床
fire-rated foam　耐火フォーム	drain pipe　排水管
conduit　溝	flow angle　流れる角度
electrical cable tube　電気配線用管	fire extinguisher　消火器
switch box　配電箱、操作ボックス	service　設備
water tank　貯水槽	

 Probably by tomorrow.
たぶん、明日までには。

防火・耐火
Fire Protection/Fire Resistance

防火・耐火性能については建材の性能面の説明だけでなく、耐用時間などの数値が重要になってきます。

examples

- The window between the kitchen and the dining room is fire-resistant.
  厨房と食堂の間の窓は耐火性能があります。

- The machinery room is enveloped with two-hour fire separation walls.
  機械室は2時間耐火壁によって囲われています。

- Special consideration has been given to fire resistance for wooden houses in the dense area.
  密集地にある住宅には特別な防火性能を施しました。

- It has become possible to erect tall fireproof timber buildings by combining steel plates.
  鉄板を組み合わせることで木構造で耐火高層木造建築が建てられるようになりました。

Quick Chat | 咄嗟のひとこと

How many hours of fire resistance is required for this wall?
この壁は何時間の耐火性能が必要ですか？

key phrases

be enveloped with~
　〜で囲われている。envelop〔名詞〕外装、〔動詞〕覆う。

two-hour fire separation walls
　2 時間耐火壁。One-hour fire-rated foam 1 時間耐火フォーム。
　The machine room requires a four-hour fire separation brick wall.
　機械室は 4 時間耐火のレンガ造の壁を必要とする。

give consideration to~
　〜を考慮する、〜に配慮する

by combining~
　〜を組み合わせることで

---

vocabulary

fire-resistant　耐火性の
machinery room　機械室
fire separation wall　耐火壁
wooden house　木造住宅
dense area　密集地

erect　立てる、建てる
fireproof　防火の
timber building　木造建築
fire-rated　耐火性の

 Two hours.
2 時間です。

断熱・換気
Heat / Insulation / Ventilation

環境負荷低減を目指す近年の建築物は、断熱、換気についての知識が求められます。数値などとともに明確な説明をする必要があります。

examples

- ► Heat insulation with 10kg/m² is installed between the external building skins.
  建物外装材の間に 10kg/m² の断熱材を採用します。

- ► An appropriate air environment can be gained by using a louver door.
  ガラリ戸を使うことで適切な空気環境を得られます。

- ► A 24-hour fan is installed in the bathroom to maintain negative pressure.
  浴室を負圧に保つために 24 時間換気扇を設置します。

- ► The southern opening has parallel louvers to prevent sunlight from directly entering the room.
  南側開口部には部屋への直射日光を防ぐため水平ルーバーを設置します。

- ► It is hard to live in a classic timber structure house due to the draughts in the winter season.
  古い木造家屋に住むと冬の隙間風が厳しい。

Quick Chat ｜咄嗟のひとこと

- Is this insulation thick enough?
  この断熱材は十分な厚さですか？

key phrases

heat insulation
断熱材。断熱材は他に thermal insulation という呼び方もある。

louver door
ガラリ戸。door leaf 扉、door frame 戸枠、door hinge 蝶番。
A door leaf with an observation window has been applied to the kitchen.
台所のドアは窓付き扉を使用した。

negative pressure
負圧。positive pressure 正圧。
This room has positive pressure to prevent cigarette smoke entering from the room nextdoor.
隣室からタバコの煙が入らないようにこの部屋は正圧とします。

it is hard to~
~することは難しい、~することは困難だ

---

vocabulary

heat insulation　断熱材
external building skin　外装
appropriate　適切な
air environment　空気環境
24-hour fan　24時間換気扇

opening　開口
parallel louvers　水平ルーバー、水平日除け
timber structure house　木造住宅
draughts　隙間風

 Yes, it meets the standards with this spec.
　はい。それはこの仕様書の基準を満たしています。

防犯・セキュリティ
Security

日本で生活する私たちには海外生活における防犯やセキュリティの重要性をイメージしづらいと思います。しかし、昨今テロの脅威にさらされる公共施設には常に防犯・セキュリティ対策が求められます。

examples

- The postbox is positioned so that the deliveryman can deliver the mail from outside.
  郵便受けは配達員が外部から投函できる場所に配置します。

- The main entrance has an auto-locking system for security reasons.
  防犯上の理由で主玄関にはオートロックがあります。

- The building manager's office has been designed to face the entrance.
  ビルの管理人室は玄関に対面して計画した。

- The emergency staircase can't be accessed from outside.
  非常階段は外部からアクセスできない。

- The elevator to the rooms is located near the reception desk.
  部屋へのエレベーターは受付デスクから近い位置としています。

- The retail shelves have been arranged so that there are no dead angles when standing at the cash counter.
  店舗の棚はレジに立ったときに死角を生まない配置とした。

Quick Chat | 咄嗟のひとこと

Q. What is the atmosphere around the site like at night?
夜間の敷地周辺はどのような雰囲気ですか？

key phrases

be positioned
配置された。be designed、be located、be arranged も同様の意味で使える。

so that~
~するように、~するために

for security reasons
防犯上の理由により
Many CCTVs are installed at the ticket hall to combat terrorism.
たくさんの監視カメラがテロ対策としてチケットホールに設置されている。

face
面する。face〔動詞〕向く。
The reception desk faces the lift hall.
受付デスクはエレベーターホールに向いています。

what is ~ like?
どんな~ですか?

---

vocabulary

postbox　郵便箱
be positioned　配置された
deliveryman　配達員
auto-locking system　オートロック
building manager's office　建物管理人室
emergency staircase　非常階段
dead angle　死角

A It is busy at weekends.
週末は騒がしいです。

51 建築環境
Architectural Environment

サステイナブル（持続可能）な建築空間を考えることが近年求められています。環境負荷低減などの取り組みが進んでいる海外のプロジェクトでは特に考慮しなければならない重要な考え方です。

examples

- The auditorium interior is covered with perforated panels to create the appropriate acoustics.
  音楽堂内部は適切な音響とするために多孔質パネルで覆います。

- The building was designed with consideration for the local climate.
  建築物はその地域の気候を考慮し、設計しました。

- The site has a warm climate that welcomes the guests.
  敷地は訪問者を迎え入れる温暖な気候に恵まれている。

- A damp-proof course has been installed between the concrete base and blockwork.
  コンクリート基礎とブロックの間に防湿処理を施しました。

- Acoustic insulation is installed behind the ceiling panels to prevent sound reflection.
  音の反響を抑えるための天井パネル裏に吸音材を張ります。

Quick Chat ｜咄嗟のひとこと

- How can we reduce echoes?
  反響を抑えるにはどうしたらいいのか？

key phrases

perforated panel
多孔質パネル。perforated acoustic board 多孔質吸音板。perforate 穴を開ける。
The builder perforated the MDF board to transform it into a noise-absorbing material.
施工者は MDF に穴を開け吸音材とした。

design with consideration for~
〜を考慮して設計する

installed between~
〜の間に設置される。installed behind~/ 〜の後ろに配置される。

acoustic insulation
吸音材。sound isolation 遮音、防音。

sound reflection
音の反響。同様の意味で acoustic reflection、echo。

reduce echo
音の反響を抑える

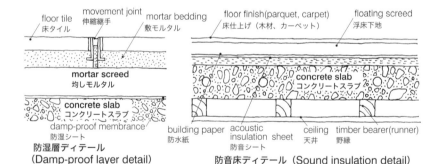

防湿層ディテール (Damp-proof layer detail)

防音床ディテール (Sound insulation detail)

---

vocabulary

auditorium　音楽堂
appropriate　適切な
acoustics　音響
warm climate　温暖な気候
welcome　迎え入れる
damp-proof layer　防湿層

concrete base　コンクリート基礎
blockwork　ブロック（でつくられたもの）
insulation　吸音材、断熱材
prevent　防ぐ、抑える

 Why don't we cover the internal wall with fabric?
壁面を布で覆ってみてはどうだろうか？

コラム①

英語に直訳する前に、まず日本語をシンプルに

　英語でプレゼン資料を作成したり、メールを書く時、建築用語の英訳がわからないことがあります。そのような時は、とりあえずネットの翻訳機能や辞書アプリ等で英訳を調べているのではないでしょうか。その時、例えば建築用語である「はめ殺し」や「取り合い」の英訳が「Fit killing」や「Struggle」と出てくれば、さすがにおかしいと気づきますが、本当に正しい英訳なのかどうかいまいち確信が持てないかもしれません。これは建築用語が日本語の中でも特殊な専門用語であるから起きる問題です。

　そんな建築用語を英語にする際、私が心がけているのは直訳するのではなく、まずは元の日本語をシンプルな日本語に和訳することでした。そのためにはその専門用語をきちんと理解していなければなりません。現場で身に着けた建築用語をいざ解説しようとすると日本語ですら言葉に詰まってしまうことがあります。

　このような時、大切なのは「結局、それはどういうことなのか？」を端的にまとめる能力と言えます。あるいは「ざっくり把握する能力」。いわゆる"意訳"と呼ばれるものです。日本語の対訳としての英語が必ずあると思い込んでしまうのは、ペーパーテストによる正解主義で教育を受けてきた日本人が陥りがちなところです。意訳を恐れてはいけません。それはクライアント自身がまとめ切れていない要望をざっくりとまとめ「あなたが求めていることはこういうことですか？」と提案するデザインの仕事に近い感覚です。

　専門用語を英訳しづらいと思ったら、まずはシンプルな日本語にしてみる。これはぜひ試してみてもらいたいと思います。

勤務先のフロアの風景。見通しの良いオフィスとは丸見えのオフィスと言えます。

Ready-to-use
Architectural
English
Expressions

STEP.2

プレゼンテーション・テクニック

Presentation Techniques

52 プレゼンテーションを始める
Starting a Presentation

プレゼンテーションは、自己紹介を兼ねた会話から始まります。その際、お決まりの会話ネタを用意しておくと、余裕が生まれ、プレゼンテーションに集中することができます。

examples

- Let me introduce her. This is Ms. Saito and she looks after the service area.
  彼女のことを紹介させてください。設備エリアを担当する齊藤さんです。

- Thank you for your time today.
  本日はお時間有難うございます。

- Thank you for the opportunity to give our presentation.
  私たちのプレゼンの機会をいただき有難うございます。

- First of all, I would like to give you a brief about the project and explain its background.
  まず最初にプロジェクトの概要と背景を説明したいと思います。

- Ok, let's move onto the next topic.
  はい、それでは次の議題に移ります。

- So, we conclude that our design would be the best option for your project.
  それゆえに、私たちのデザインが皆様の計画にとって一番の選択だと結論付けます。

🏆 Quick Chat ｜咄嗟のひとこと

Q Nice to meet you, Mr. Ito.
始めまして伊東さん。

key phrases

let me~
～させてください。let me begin with~/ ～から始めさせてください、let me explain about~/ ～について説明させてください、などはプレゼンの場で使いやすい。

look after~
～の面倒を見る、～の世話をする、～を担当する。類似表現に take cafe of~。

give a presentation
プレゼンテーションする

first of all
まず始めに。いくつかの議題のある時の最初に取りかかるときに使う。

give a brief
概要を説明する

explain the background
背景を説明する

move onto the next
次へ移る

would be the best option
きっと最良の選択肢だろう。would be ~/ きっと～だろう。

---

vocabulary

introduce	紹介する	topic	議題、話題
opportunity	機会	conclude	結論付ける
brief	概要	option	選択肢
background	背景		

 Hi! Please call me Toyo.
どうも、豊雄と呼んでください。

53 提案する
Proposing Ideas

アイデアやデザインを自分たちの利益のためだけに提案するのではなく、相手にとっても有益になる話をしたいものです。その結果、共感が得られ、通りやすい提案となるはずです。

examples

- The architectural plans have been evolved in this way for the following reasons.
  この建築計画は次のような理由から導き出されました。

- Why don't we choose the alternative idea?
  もう一つの案を選んでみたらどうだろうか？

- We recommend this product for these reasons.
  私たちはこれらの理由で、この製品を推薦します。

- We recommend plan A if you wish to gain more attention from potential customers.
  もし潜在的な顧客からより注目を集めたいのであれば、私たちはA案をお勧めします。

- We have another option to offer you since our previous meeting, as outlined below.
  私たちの前回の打ち合わせから、以下の概略のとおりもう一つの案を提案します。

Quick Chat | 咄嗟のひとこと

- Shall we propose another idea?
  さらなるアイデアを提案しましょうか？

key phrases

for the following reason
次の理由で。プレゼン、書類、メールなどでも、まず最初に結論を伝え、その後に結論に至った理由を説明する。
We decided to proceed with plan A for the following reasons.
私たちは以下の理由からA案で進めることを決めました。

why don't we~?
~したらどうだろうか? そこから、~しましょう、という自分たちへの提案として使う。Why don't you~? ~をしてはいかがですか? 相手に対しての提案として使う。

if you wish to~
もし~したいなら、もし~を望むなら

gain more attention from~
~の注意をひく。pay attention to~/ ~へ注意を払う。

as outlined below
以下の概略のとおり、次の概略のとおり

narrow ~ down
~を絞る、~を狭める、~を厳選する

---

vocabulary

alternative	代わりの	option	選択肢
recommend	推薦する	offer	提案する、提供する
attention	注目、注意	since~	~以来
potential customers	潜在的顧客	previous	以前の
another	もう一つの		

 No, we should rather narrow them down.
いや、逆に絞るべきだ。

54 根拠・理由・例を示す
Giving Reasons and Examples

話し合いを進める際、客観的なデータ等を提示した上で根拠や理由を説明することが大切です。それを元に話し合いを進めていけば相手も納得の上、判断してくれるでしょう。

examples

▶ We identified three distinguishing characteristics after analyzing the town.
この街は3つの優れた特徴を持つと分析しました。

▶ The location of access points to the building was based on the shape of the site parameter.
建物へのアクセス動線は敷地形状を根拠にしました。

▶ We should refer to a mature city where a similar event has already been held.
似たイベントを既に開催した成熟都市を参照すべきです。

▶ Why don't you explore the concept together with other options at the actual site?
現地で他のオプションと共にコンセプトを検討してはいかがでしょうか？

▶ We have terminated our selection process for these reasons.
このような理由で私たちの選考過程を終えた。

🍷 **Quick Chat** ｜咄嗟のひとこと

Q: Do you think they understand with this example?
その例で彼らは理解すると思いますか？

key phrases

distinguishing
優れた。distinguish〔動詞〕見分ける、特徴づける。似た意味に define。
The activities of the visitors define the character of the space.
訪問者の活動が空間を特徴づけます。

analyze
分析する。似た意味では research、investigate、study。名詞形は analysis 分析。
We attach this analysis as an appendix.
私たちはこの分析を付属資料として添付します。

based on~
〜を根拠に、〜をもとに

explore the concept
コンセプトを検討する

together with~
〜とともに、〜と一緒に

at the actual site
現地で

for these reasons
このような理由で

might be~
〜かもしれない

---

vocabulary

identify　認識する	mature city　成熟都市
distinguishing　突出した、優れた	similar　似た
analyze　分析する	explore　検討する、探求する
the shape of　〜の形	appendix　付属資料、付属物、別表
site parameter　敷地境界	

 It might be difficult for Europeans to understand.
　　ヨーロッパ人には理解しづらいかもしれません。

強調する・比べる・言い換える
Emphasizing/Comparing/Paraphrasing

1つの例でいくら強調しても伝わりにくい場面がありますが、他の例と比較したり、別の表現で言い換えると、伝わりやすくなります。

examples

- We consider that the site is slightly different from typical tourist sites.
  私たちはこの敷地を典型的な観光地とは微妙に異なると考えます。

- In comparison to other firms' proposals, we have made our plan more compact.
  他の事務所の案と比較して、私たちの案はよりコンパクトにまとめました。

- This plan can shorten the construction period. In other words, it can reduce the cost.
  この案だと工期を短くできます。言い換えれば、費用を少なくできるのです。

- The contrast will be increased by inserting glass boxes into the brickwork building.
  レンガ造建築にガラスの箱を挿入することでコントラストが強くなるでしょう。

- The revised areas on the drawings are highlighted with red lines.
  図面の修正部分は赤線で強調されています。

Quick Chat | 咄嗟のひとこと

Q How do we emphasize this sentence?
どのようにこの文章を強調しますか？

key phrases

slightly different from~
～と微妙に異なる。～と多少違う。反対語に huge difference、big difference 大きな違い。

in comparison to~
～と比較して。compare to~/ ～と比較する。compare A with B は A を B と比較する。

make a plan compact
案や計画をコンパクトにする、簡潔な案・計画にまとめる

shorten the period
期間を短縮する

in other words
言い換えると、すなわち。類語として that is to say。

The building should be sustainable. That is to say, architects have to consider maintenance very carefully.
建物は持続可能性がなければならない。すなわち建築家は維持管理をしっかりと考えなければならない。

reduce the cost
コストを削減する、コストを下げる

---

vocabulary

slightly 多少、微妙に	insert 挿入する
comparison 比較	revised 訂正された
firm 会社	drawing 図面
shorten 短くする	highlight 強調する
contrast 対比	emphasize 強調する
increase 増加する	

 We should change to bold gothic lettering.
太字のゴシック体に変えるべきでしょう。

将来の話をする
Talking about the Future

建築は完成した時点がゴールではありません。使われ始めてからが大切です。依頼者や利用者と使われ方の情報を共有する配慮が必要です。

examples

- Our proposal reveals the potential tourism resources of this town.
  私たちの提案はこの街の潜在的観光資源を顕在化します。

- We expect the amount of visitors to increase three times more in five years.
  私たちは訪問者数がこの5年間で3倍以上増加すると見込んでいます。

- Historical buildings would make for a good legacy if preserved.
  歴史的建物は保全されれば良き遺産となるでしょう。

- The service room is situated in the area at the back of house to allow for the upgrading of machinery.
  設備室は機種更新のためにバックヤードに計画します。

- The floor detail proposes a raised access floor to update the office layout.
  床のディテールはオフィスレイアウトの更新のために上げ床を提案します。

- We have also considered sustainability in the proposal. The issue of running costs, for example.
  この提案は持続可能性も考えました。例えば、ランニングコストの問題のような。

Quick Chat | 咄嗟のひとこと

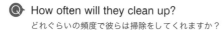

How often will they clean up?
どれぐらいの頻度で彼らは掃除をしてくれますか？

key phrases

increase three times more
3倍に増える。増加するには enlarge、grow、rise など。2倍は twice もしくは twofold。
If we get the site nextdoor, the scale of the project will increase twofold.
もし私たちが隣の敷地を獲得できたら、計画が2倍に増えます。

in five years
5年間で。似た意味で within もあるが、より厳密な意味合いになる。
We will complete the set of drawings within a week.
私たちは1週間以内に図面セットを仕上げます。

make for a good legacy
良い遺産となる

allow for~
〜を見込む、〜のために

issue of~
〜の問題、〜の課題。problem、trouble は悩ましい問題。issue は議論すべき課題というニュアンスがあるため、ことを大きくしたくない場合に使うと良い。

---

vocabulary

reveal	明かす、見せる、浮き彫りにする
potential	可能性のある、潜在的な
resource	資源
expect	期待する、見込む
amount of	〜の量、〜の数
increase	増加する
three times	3倍
legacy	レガシー、遺産
preserve	保全する、保存する、保護する
back of house	バックヤード
upgrade	アップグレードする、向上する、更新する
raised access floor	上げ床
update	新しくする、更新する
running costs	ランニングコスト、維持費
clean up	掃除する

 They'll clean once a week.
1週間に1回です。

57 実現可能性
Feasibility

プロジェクトの出発点で計画が曖昧だったり方向性が間違っていると後々に大きなロスとなります。プロジェクト初期段階では簡潔で的確な表現が求められます。

examples

- Although complex, the idea was examined from several aspects, such as construction costs and schedule etc.
  複雑ですが、この考えは建設費用や工期など様々な側面から検討されました。

- To what extent is this idea possible at the moment?
  現時点で、この案の可能性はどれぐらいでしょうか？

- An idea has come to my mind.
  アイデアをちょっと思いつきました。

- The idea is brilliant, but we simultaneously have to analyze whether it is feasible or not.
  アイデアは素晴らしいのですが、同時に実現可能かどうか分析しなければなりません。

- The current option for the stadium can fit the requirements for the cost and schedule.
  現在のスタジアム案は、費用と工期の要望の範囲内に収められます。

Quick Chat | 咄嗟のひとこと

What is the most important thing about studying feasibility?
実現可能性を検討するうえで最も大切なことはなんですか？

key phrases

although~
~ではあるけれど。even though、though も同じ意味。

from several aspects
様々な観点から

such as~
例えば~。for example、for instance も同じ意味。書類には e.g.(ラテン語の exempli gratia の略)という略語が出てくることもある。

at the moment
現時点で。for now や at present という類語もある。

come to one's mind
思い浮かぶ。何か思いつきを説明する際に使うと便利。
It just came to my mind.
ちょっと思いついたんだけれど。

fit the requirements
要望に沿う、要求に応える

---

vocabulary

complex	複雑な	simultaneously	同時に
examine	検討する、調査する	analyze	分析する
several	様々な	feasible	実現可能な
aspect	側面、状況	current	現在の
extent	程度	fit	収まる
brilliant	素晴らしい	requirement	要望

 To have as many options as possible?
どれだけの選択肢を作れるかでは？

コストの説明をする
Explaining the Cost

建築計画には常にお金の話題が付いて回ります。それゆえ、コストについて曖昧なまま計画を進めていくと後ほどトラブルになりかねません。関係者とは文章などでコストについて確認しておきましょう。

examples

- The maintenance costs for the current plan might be higher after completion.
  現行案での維持費は、完成後により多くかかるかも知れません。

- We have to think about the time and cost of renovating the old building before the project starts.
  古い建物を改修する前に、時間とお金について考えなければならない。

- The most important thing about communal facilities is to also think of a business plan.
  公共施設で最も重要なことは事業計画も考えることです。

- The critical point to consider about this commercial building is how to gain a higher rental income.
  この商業施設について考える上で重要な点は、どのようにしてより高い家賃を得るかです。

- The rentable floor area ratio is one of the targets for profitability.
  レンタブル比は収益性の一つの指針である。

Quick Chat | 咄嗟のひとこと

Have the tenants in this building been decided?
この施設のテナントは決まったのですか？

key phrases

maintenance costs
維持費。コスト関連の用語は次のように様々ある。service cost 設備費、construction cost 建設費、demolition cost 解体費、planning cost, design fee 設計費、research cost 研究費、rental income 家賃収入、rent〔名詞〕家賃、〔動詞〕有料で貸す、lend 無料で貸す、lease 有料＋契約して貸す、borrow 無料で貸りる。

Can we rent a car to visit the site?
敷地を訪れるために車を借りることはできますか？

the most important thing about～
～について最も大切なこと

the critical point is～
重要な点は～だ

gain a rental income
家賃収入を得る

the target for～
～の指針

---

vocabulary

maintenance cost　維持費
current plan　現在の案、現行案
after completion　完成後に、竣工後に
renovate　改修する
communal facility　公共施設
business plan　事業計画

critical　重要な
rentable floor area ratio　レンタブル比
target　指針、目的
profitability　収益性

 One of them will be a Japanese restaurant.
一つは和食レストランだそうです。

59 メンテナンスへの配慮を説明する
Explaining Maintenance Arrangements

建設費を抑えられても、メンテナンスにお金がかかっては良い建築とは言えません。明快でシンプルなメンテナンス計画が設計に組み込まれていれば、プロジェクト実現に向けて良いアピールになるはずです。

examples

- Artificial leaves are used as a green wall for easier maintenance.
  より簡単な維持管理のために人工葉を壁面緑化に使用している。

- The mechanical service rooms are directly accessible from outside to make inspection easy.
  機械設備室は点検をより簡単にするために外部から直接アクセスできます。

- The circulation in the electrical room has been carefully laid out to facilitate monthly inspection.
  電気室内の動線は毎月一回の点検のために十分計画された。

- The method for replacing light bulbs should be proposed together with the atrium ceiling design.
  照明電球の交換方法は吹き抜け天井のデザインと一緒に提案されなければならない。

- The cleaning method for glass in high-rise buildings should be considered.
  高層ビルのガラスのクリーニング方法は考慮されていなければならない。

Quick Chat | 咄嗟のひとこと

Q. Why did you choose that tile?
何故そのタイルを選んだのですか？

key phrases

be used as~
〜として使われる。usable 使うことのできる。usable area 有効面積。usability 使い勝手、使いやすさ。

The gray colored door is used as a fire separation door.
灰色のドアは防火扉として使用されています。

make inspection easy
点検をしやすくする、点検しやすいように

be carefully laid out
丁寧に計画された、十分に計画された

monthly inspection
毎月の点検。site observation 現場監理、現場視察。site visit 現場視察。weekly coordination meeting 毎週の定例会議。every month 毎月。once a month 月一回。

should be~
〜すべき、〜であるべき。様々な現場で多用する表現。

The size of the window should be decided by tomorrow.
窓のサイズは明日までに決めなければならない。

together with~
〜と一緒に

vocabulary

artificial leaves 人工緑葉	electrical room 電気室
green wall/wall greening 壁面緑化	facilitate 容易にする、円滑にする
	monthly 月一の、毎月の
mechanical service room 機械設備室	method 方法
	replace 交換する
directly 直接に	light bulb 電球
accessible アクセス可能な	atrium ceiling 吹き抜け天井
inspection 検査、点検	high-rise building 高層ビル
circulation 動線	

 Because it has high maintainability.
なぜならメンテナンス性に優れているからです。

オプションを提示する
Proposing Options

一つのアイデアを磨き上げるとともに、あらゆる方向から検証し、検討の余地がないか考えます。別の選択肢を提示する柔軟さを併せ持つことも設計者に必要な能力です。

examples

- This version reduces the cost of the previous proposal.
  今回の案は前回の案に比べてコストを抑えられます。

- Option A was rejected for maintenance reasons. How about option B, then?
  A案が維持管理の理由で不採用でした。ではB案はいかがでしょうか？

- Rather than presenting you with many options, today we have brought the proposal we think is the best.
  いくつも選択肢を提示するよりも、本日は私たちの一押しの案を持参しました。

- We should prepare three options and include one challenging option among more conventional ones.
  3つの選択肢を準備し、普通の案の中に挑戦的な案を1つ混ぜるべきです。

- We will change the meeting room due to overbooking.
  オーバーブッキングのため会議室を変更いたします。

Quick Chat | 咄嗟のひとこと

Q Which one shall we choose, plan A or plan B?
A案、B案、どちらを選びましょうか？

key phrases

reduce the cost
コストを削減する

reject
拒否する。rejection letter 不採用通知。rejected applicant 不採用者。類似表現に deny 否定する。
My idea was denied by the project leader.
私の案はプロジェクトリーダーに否定された。

how about ~, then?
それでは~はどうか？
前文を受けて、他の選択肢などを提示するときに使う構文。
I like Le Corbusier. How about you?
私はル・コルビュジエが好きです。あなたはどうですか？（同じ話題を相手に振るときに使える）

rather than ~ ing
~するよりも
Rather than demolishing this house, why don't you refurbish it?
この家を壊すよりも、改修してはどうですか？

the proposal we think is the best
私たちがベストだと思う提案

---

vocabulary

version　バージョン、版、種類	option　選択肢
previous　以前の	bring　持参する
prepare　準備する	among~　~の中の
include　含める	conventional　普通の
challenging　挑戦的な	overbooking　オーバーブッキング

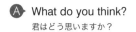
What do you think?
君はどう思いますか？

メリット・デメリットを説明する
Explaining the Advantages and Disadvantages

自分たちの提案を進める際、メリットばかりを説明しがちですが、敢えてデメリット（対処法とともに）を伝えることで関係者からの信頼を得るだけでなく、余計な指摘を受けることもありません。

examples

- This is our proposal based on our investigation of the pros and cons.
  これはメリット・デメリットのどちらも検討した上でのご提案です。

- The current changes produce not only benefits but also losses.
  現時点での変更は利益を生み出すだけでなく、損失にもなります。

- The wall color will be much brighter, but the residents may still feel uncomfortable.
  壁面の色は大変明るくなるが、住人は落ち着かないかもしれない。

- While it is difficult to maintain green walls, they reduce heat on buildings.
  壁面緑化の維持管理は難しいが、建物の熱を抑えます。

- This option is good for the surrounding scenery but bad for maintenance.
  この案は周囲の景観に対して良いが、メンテナンス性が悪い。

- Renovation of the building will be good for the townscape. However, it might cost as much as a brand new building.
  改修だと街の景観に優しくなるでしょう。しかし、費用は新築を建てる時と同じかもしれない。

Quick Chat ｜咄嗟のひとこと

Q: Do we need to explain the disadvantages?
デメリットを説明する必要があるのですか？

key phrases

a proposal based on one's investigation
〜を検討したうえでの提案。類似表現に a proposal made after investigating〜 もある。

pros and cons
良い点と悪い点。advantage 利点、disadvantage 不利な点（メリット・デメリットに相当する単語）。
We will show the disadvantages of our proposal at present.
現時点での私たちの案のデメリットを紹介します。

not only benefits but also losses
利益だけでなく、損失も。利益には gain や profit や revenue など。損失には disbenefit、negative profit など。

feel uncomfortable
居心地が悪い、落ち着かない

vocabulary

investigation 検討	it is difficult to〜 〜するのは難しい
pros and cons メリット・デメリット	surrounding scenery 周囲の景観
current changes 現時点での変更	renovation 改修
benefits and losses 利益と損失	townscape 町の景観
brighter より明るい	as much as〜 〜と同じ量の
uncomfortable 居心地のよくない	brand new building 新築

 Why not?
はい。(なぜしないんだ？ 肯定的な意味合いで Yes の意味)

質問をする
Asking Questions

適切な質問をすることでしか、適切な回答は得られません。しかも英語での混乱を避けるためにもなるべく少ないやり取りでコミュニケーションをしたいものです。

examples

- That's all from us. Any questions?
  私たちからは以上です。質問などありますか？

- Do you mind if we ask a question?
  私たちから一つ質問がありますが、よろしいでしょうか？

- Do you have any other queries?
  その他に質問などありますか？

- The application says to print on both sides of the paper. So, does the requested number refer to the sheets of paper or the pages?
  応募要項には両面刷りとありました。それでは指定のページ数とは紙の枚数？ もしくはページ数？

- First of all, we will explain our proposal. Then, if necessary, we will answer your questions.
  まず初めに私たちの提案を説明します。その後に必要ならば皆様の質問を受けます。

Quick Chat ｜咄嗟のひとこと

Sorry to disturb you, but can I have a minute?
邪魔してすみませんが、ちょっと数分よろしいでしょうか？

key phrases

that's all
これで終わりです。

do you mind if~?
～してもよろしいでしょうか？
Do you mind if I ask a question ?
質問しても良いですか？
No, I don't mind.
質問をしても気にしない（すなわち"質問しても OK！"という意味）

say~
～とある。say は「人が～と言う」が一般的だが、書類などに「～と書いてある」という意味でも使う。
The competiton brief says all applicants should be registered online.
コンペティションの要項にすべての応募者はオンライン上で登録されていなければならない、とあります。

print on both sides of the paper
両面に印刷する

refer to~
～のことを指す、～に言及する

if necessary
もし必要ならば。類似表現に if required。if requested もし要望されているならば。if you need もしあなたが必要とするならば。
We don't mind showing our proposal now if required.
もし必要ならば私たちの案を今お見せしても構いませんよ。

---

vocabulary

query　質問、要望
application　応募要項
sheet of paper　用紙、紙

necessary　必要な
answer questions　質問を受ける

 Sure.
もちろん。

即答を避ける
Avoiding a Quick Response

プレゼンテーションにおける不測の事態や突然の質問に対しては、常に決まったフレーズを用意しておきます。そのフレーズを挟むことでワンクッションを置き、時間稼ぎながら、回答を考えることができます。

examples

- Well, our presentation slides haven't loaded yet. Please give us a moment.
  あれ、スライドがまだ立ち上がりません、少しお待ちください。

- More detailed information is required, so I will take this issue back to the office and check.
  もう少し詳細な情報が必要なので、この問題を事務所に持ち帰り、調べます。

- That is a good question. Do you mind if I have some time to think about it?
  それは大変良い指摘です。ちょっと考える時間をいただけますか?

- Ms. Sejima would know more about this issue than me. I will let her know when I get back to my office.
  その問題については私より妹島が詳しく知っています。帰社したら彼女に伝えます。

- I just noticed that this document is out of date.
  この資料が古いことに今、気付きました。

- Is it OK to circulate the latest version of this information to team members by email after the meeting?
  この最新情報を会議後にメンバーにメールで回覧してもよろしいでしょうか?

- We might need to make a further study of the building shape due to changes in the budget.
  予算の変更に伴い、建物形状のさらなるスタディが必要になるかもしれません。

Quick Chat | 咄嗟のひとこと

- Well, there is something wrong…
  あれ、ちょっと様子がおかしいようです。

key phrases

give a moment
少々お時間をください（お待ちくださいの意味）。同じ意味で Give us a second、Just a moment, please、Wait a moment, Hang on a sec などがある。電話口で少々お待ちくださいは、Please hold the line や Hold on a sec など。

take ~ back and check
～を持ち帰って調べる、～を持ち帰って確認する

get back to~
～に帰る。似た表現で go back to~ など。
When will the project manager come back to the office?
いつ頃、プロジェクトマネージャーは帰社しますか？

out of date
期限切れ。古いことを意味する。関連表現に the most up-to-date information、the latest information ともに「最新情報」の意味。due date 期限。issue date 発行日。

circulate A to B
AをBに回覧する。配布するという意味では distribute A to B がある。
Would you distribute the meeting agenda to all participants before the meeting?
会議前に会議の議題を全参加者に配布してもらえませんか？

---

vocabulary

slide	スライド	let~know	～に教える
load	（機器やソフトが）立ち上がる	document	書類
detailed information	詳細情報	the latest version of~	～の最新版

 Ok, why don't we change the order?
じゃあ、順番を変えますか？

締めくくる
Concluding Business

その打ち合わせの結果と次回の話し合いまでに各自がやるべきことなど、皆が顔を合わせる場所での終わり方、締めくくり方は非常に大切です。曖昧な点がなくなるまで確認します。

examples

- In conclusion, our retail design must be the best option to suit your company's philosophy.
  結論として、私たちの店舗デザインが御社の理念に対して一番ふさわしい案に違いありません。

- That is all from us.
  私たちからは以上です。

- That is all from the meeting agenda. Does anyone have anything else to share?
  会議の議題からは以上です。誰か他になにか報告することはありますか？

- I am afraid we don't have much time. This will be the last question.
  残念ですが、あまり時間がありません。これが最後の質問となります。

- It is getting dark, so we should finish our site survey soon.
  暗くなってきたので現地調査をまもなく終わりにしましょう。

Quick Chat | 咄嗟のひとこと

Do you have any other topics to discuss?
他に議論すべきトピックありますか？

key phrases

in conclusion
結論として。似た表現で consequently などがある。
Consequently, this option is the most profitable.
結局、この選択肢が一番収益を生みます。

be best suited
最もふさわしい

that is all
以上です。似た表現で That's it などがある。for now を最後に付けると「今のところ以上です」となる。
Is there anything else? That is all for now.
他に何かありますか？　今のところ以上です。

have something to share
報告すること（共有しておくこと）。類似表現に A.O.B (Any Other Business) その他の議題。

I'm afraid that〜
残念ですが〜

---

vocabulary

conclusion　結論
philosophy　哲学
agenda　議題
be afraid that〜　残念ながら〜、〜であることは残念です

dark　暗い
site survey　現地調査
finish soon　すぐに終わる
profitable　有益な

 Can I confirm one point?
1点、確認させてください。

コンペティションへの応募
Entry to a Competition

コンペの応募に関しては、単にこちらの熱意を訴えかけて参加するのではなく、参加することが主催者にとっても有益になるであろうことをきちんと説明することが望ましいでしょう。

examples

- We would like to confirm whether the scale of our company makes us eligible to apply to this competition.
  このコンペティションに弊社の規模でも応募可能か確認したい。

- Can we enter work made in collaboration with the local qualified architects?
  私たちが現地の登録建築士と協働した作品で参加することは可能ですか？

- When will detailed information be uploaded to the website?
  いつ、詳細情報がウェブサイトにアップされますか？

- Relevant projects within the last five years are included in this portfolio.
  このポートフォリオには最近5年以内の関連プロジェクトが含まれています。

- Some images are inserted into the project brief.
  プロジェクト概要にいくつか画像が挿入されています。

- This project is noted in my project experience even though it was carried out under my previous firm.
  このプロジェクトは以前の勤務先で私が担当したので、実務経験として記載します。

Quick Chat | 咄嗟のひとこと

- Will you submit your work?
  あなたの作品で応募しますか？

key phrases

apply to~
〜に応募する

in collaboration with~
〜と協働する。work together with~/ 〜と一緒に働く。
Can we work together with them even though we have different cultural backgrounds?
私たちに異なる文化背景があっても彼らと一緒に働けますでしょうか？

qualified architect
資格のある建築士。日本では一級建築士などのこと。registered architect や chartered architect も似たような意味。

be uploaded to~
〜にアップロードされた。サイトにファイルをアップロードする。オンラインサーバーへの保存や SNS などに投稿する際に使う。
Please don't upload any project information, text, image or movie onto SNS before the bulding opens.
建物がオープンする前にこの計画の情報を文字、画像、動画として SNS にアップしないでください。

within the last ~ years
最近〜年以内で

---

vocabulary

confirm whether~ 〜かどうか確認する	upload to~ 〜にアップロードする
be eligible to~ 〜できる、可能である	relevant 関連した
competition コンペティション、競技、競争	insert 挿入する
	project brief プロジェクト概要
enter 参加する	be noted 記載されている
collaborate 協働する	project experience 実務経験
qualified 資格のある、認められた	even though~ 〜だけれども
detailed information 詳細情報	previous firm 以前の職場

A Let me think about it.
ちょっと検討させてください。

提案書の作成
Creating a Proposal Document

提案書だけでなく、パネルや図面上では図版が主役であり、文章は補助として考えます。英語での表現は極力優しい単語でシンプルに表現するのが良いでしょう。

examples

- The drawings were arranged in landscape format in order to incorporate the surrounding conditions of the site.
  図面は敷地周辺条件を取り込みやすいように横レイアウトとしました。

- The pages of the application need blank space on the binding side.
  申請書のページは綴じる側に余白が必要となります。

- We were requested to mount the drawings on board so that they can be stood against the wall.
  壁に立てかけやすいように図面をボード張りにするよう求められた。

- How do we display facing pages on this screen?
  この画面にページを見開きで表示させるにはどうしたらいい？

- First, I'll send a brief summary of the submission by email attachment.
  まず応募案の概要をメールに添付してお送ります。

- The high-resolution original file will be uploaded to an online server.
  オンラインサーバー上に高画質の原本ファイルを保存しておきます。

Quick Chat ｜咄嗟のひとこと

Q. How do we show within the judging process?
   審査過程においてはどのように見せますか？

key phrases

arrange in landscape format
（紙面や画面で）横レイアウトとする。horizontal 横、portrait 縦レイアウト、vertical 縦。

bind
製本する。bind the document 書類を綴じる。twin-loop bound document ダブルリング製本された資料。staple ホッチキスで留める。stapler ホッチキス。

mount ~ on board
～をボード貼りにする

stand against the wall
壁に立てかかる

facing pages
見開きページ。single page 片ページ。

brief summary
概要。似た表現で overview、description、outline、synopsis。
Is it possible for you to send us the outline of the project first?
まず初めに計画の概要を私たちに送ることは可能ですか？

by email attachment
メールに添付して

---

vocabulary

drawing　図面
incorporate　取り込む
surrounding conditions　周辺条件
application　申請書
blank space　余白

binding　製本
submission　応募案、提出物
high-resolution　高解像度
original　原案、原物、オリジナル
online server　オンラインサーバー

 We should put numbers on the boards.
パネルに番号を入れて置こう。

プレゼン用データの作成
Creating Presentation Data

スライドを使ったプレゼンでは相手からの視点でどのように見えるのかを考えることが大切です。特に不慣れな言語を使うのならば、スライドにはキャッチコピーのような短いフレーズに絞り、極力グラフィックで説明する方法もあります。

examples

▶ The drawings that have just been pasted on the slides are illegible.
ただスライドに貼りつけられた図面は読めません。

▶ The way it looks in the drawings and in the slides is totally different.
図面上とスライド上の見え方は全然違います。

▶ We have to think about how the slides will look when projected on the screen.
スクリーンに映し出されるスライドの見え方を考えなければならない。

▶ The slide order doesn't have to be the same as the creative process.
スライドの順番は制作過程と必ずしも同じである必要はない。

▶ We have to edit the PPT slides before the final presentation.
私たちは最終プレゼンの前に PPT スライドを編集しなければならない。

💡 **Quick Chat** | 咄嗟のひとこと

Why don't we switch the first and second slides?
一枚目と二枚目のスライドを入れ替えたらどうだろうか？

key phrases

paste on~
〜に貼る。関連表現に copy and paste コピペ、cut and paste 切り貼り、duplicate 複製する、delete, eliminate 消去する、move 移動する、switch, swap 入れ替える。

the way it looks
見え方。how it will look 見え方。どう見えるか。

be totally different
全然違う、全く異なる

project
投影する。project は計画〔名詞〕の他に、動詞としてもよく使う。projector プロジェクター（映写機）。

Shall we bring our own portable projector to the presentation?
プレゼンテーションに自前の携帯プロジェクターを持参しましょうか？

PPT slide
パワーポイントのスライド。他の主なソフトウェアのファイル名は、AI file イラストレーターファイル、Word file ワードファイル、Excel file エクセルファイル、attached PDF file 添付 PDF ファイル。

I will give a presentation using a PDF file in full screen mode.
私は PDF ファイルの全画面表示でプレゼンテーションを行います。

---

vocabulary

paste 貼る	be the same as~ 〜と同様に
illegible 判読しにくい	creative process 制作過程
totally 全体的に、全くもって	edit 編集
order 順番	final 最後の

 No, we should delete both.
いや、両方とも削るべきです。

プレスリリースで使う表現
Expressions for Press Release

プレスリリースを作成するときには該当プロジェクトの5W1Hをリストアップし、それを元に簡潔な文章を作成すれば受け手に取ってわかり易い、すなわち伝わりやすい情報を提供できるはずです。

examples

- Yama Architects is delighted to introduce its latest project, designed and supervised on site.
  このたび山嵜建築設計事務所が設計・監理を行った最新の建物が竣工しましたことをお知らせします。

- Our client has courteously permitted us to hold a private view.
  クライアントのご厚意により、内覧会を開催します。

- The project site is in a downtown district of Tokyo left over from redevelopment of the area.
  計画地は東京の再開発から取り残された下町地域にあります。

- The project was started with the motivation to create a new cityscape in front of the station.
  本計画は駅前に新しい都市の風景を生み出すという動機で始まりました。

- We collaborated with local architects on this project.
  私たちは本計画において現地の建築士と協働しました。

- It would be appreciated if you could join us at the opening party and give us your comments.
  オープニングパーティーにご参加いただき、ご批評賜れば幸いです。

Quick Chat ｜咄嗟のひとこと

Q: Do we have too much information?
情報量が多くないか？

key phrases

be delighted to~
〜して嬉しい。似た表現に be pleased to announce お知らせできて嬉しい。be glad to inform you 情報を提供できてうれしい。be happy to tell you お伝えできて嬉しい。

design and supervise on site
設計・監理を行う

be left over from~
〜から取り残された

with the motivation to~
〜しようという動機で

it would be appreciated if~
〜していただけると幸いです。要望を伝えるための非常に丁寧な表現。

vocabulary

introduce A to B　A を B に紹介する	redevelopment　再開発
the latest　最新の	start with~　〜で始める
courteously　厚意で	motivation　動機
hold　開催する	cityscape　街並み
private view　内覧会	give comments　批評する、感想を言う、意見を言う
downtown district　下町地域	

 Let's put it together onto a single A4 sheet.
A4 一枚にまとめましょう。

コラム②

> プレゼン。相手の目線で考える。

　ロンドンの設計事務所に勤務していたとき、様々な企業の説明資料や建材メーカーのカタログを見る機会がありました。そこで気づいたのは、日本企業が発行する企業紹介やカタログには分かりづらいものが多かった、ということです。しかし、それは英語力の問題というより、その企業や商品が何を伝えたいか、というメッセージが弱いことに起因していると思いました。これは主語が無くても文章が成立し、曖昧な文章が生まれてしまう日本語の弱点とも言えます。

　企業の特徴や売れ筋商品を冒頭できっちりアピールしてくる他の資料に比べ、挨拶文や企業設立の歴史背景を延々と説明するページはどうしても読む気がしません。プレゼンを考えるときに日本語で響かなければ、それをいくら美しい英語で表現したところで世界の舞台では伝わらないと思います。

　また、プレゼンをする際に大切なのは、明確な日本語とそれを意訳する英語スキルだけではありません。建築業界で働く私たちには、図面、グラフィック、模型などという言葉を交わさずとも世界中の同業者とコミュニケーションできるツールを持ち合わせています。英語だけでなくそれらを駆使し相手の注意を引くやり方も十分有効です。英語に不自由を感じるからこそ、表現がシンプルになり、洗練されてくることもあります。実はその単語に言いたいことの本質が詰まっていたりするのです。

　いくらそのデザインに思い入れがあったとしても、結局は相手がそれをどのように見るかがカギであり、それが客観性に繋がっていきます。それが相手の目線で考える、ということなのです。

模型室での風景。模型などをうまく駆使すれば英語力をカバーできます。

Ready-to-use
Architectural
English
Expressions

STEP.3

現場のコミュニケーション

Communication in Practice

資料の確認・受け渡し
Confirming the Document and Handing it Over

図面や資料の受け渡しなどはメールや郵便で送った後、届いているかどうか確認することで時間のロスを防げます。相手が忙しくて届いているのに確認しないこともありますし、紛失していることもあります。

examples

- Please write the revision notes and issuer's initials clearly.
  図面の改訂履歴と記載者のイニシャルをハッキリと書いてください。

- Please don't forget the drawing scale, orientation and also the grid numbers.
  グリッド番号同様、図面縮尺、方位を忘れずに。

- Have you checked the drawing attached to the email sent this morning?
  今朝送ったメールの添付図面見ましたか？

- The images and drawings will be sent by email as attachments.
  写真や図面は添付してメールで送ります。

- The information requested is too large to attach to emails.
  要望された資料はファイルサイズが非常に大きく、メールに添付できません。

- Alternatively, we will save the files onto an online server.
  代わりに、ファイルはオンラインサーバーに保存します。

Quick Chat ｜咄嗟のひとこと

Q: Have you booked the courier?
宅配便の手配はしましたか？

key phrases

revision note
改訂履歴。「図面が最新版であるのか?」「議題になっている図面が同じ図面なのか?」それを知る手掛かりが改訂版記録です。日付と担当者名も一緒に伝えておけば混乱を減らせます。省略形は Rev. となります。

have you checked~?
~をチェックしましたか? 類似表現に Have you received~?/ ~は届きましたか? Have you opened the email?/ メールを開きましたか?

send as an attachment
添付として送る。attach 添付する。
Please find the attached drawings.
添付された図面をご覧ください。

save onto an online server
オンラインサーバーに保存する

---

vocabulary

revision 改訂	grid number グリッド番号
issuer 提出者、記載者、発行人	attachment 添付物
initial イニシャル	alternatively 代わりに、代替として
clearly 明確に、はっきりと	book 予約する、手配する
drawing scale 図面縮尺	courier 宅配便
orientation 方位	

 Yes, he will arrive soon.
はい、間もなく到着します。

お願いの仕方
How to Make a Request

お願いする際は相手の置かれている状況を見極めましょう。相手が忙しい時や機嫌が悪い時などは避けるべきです。お願いの内容よりもお願いする状況やタイミングによって、通るかどうかが決まることが多いです。

examples

- Could you say that again?
  もう一度お聞かせ願えませんか？

- It would be much appreciated if you could contact the contractor directly.
  施工業者と直接やり取りしていただけると大変助かります。

- We always need the most up-to-date drawings on site.
  現場では常に最新の図面を必要としています。

- Would it be possible to have an opportunity to make a presentation?
  私たちにプレゼンテーションの機会をいただくことは可能ですか？

- Could you please send us the tile samples from the local factory?
  現地の工場からタイルサンプルを私たちに送ってもらえませんか？

- Please send the CAD drawings following the right procedure afterwards.
  後ほど正しい手順でCAD図面を送ってください。

- Could you resend the file saved in the former version, please?
  以前のバージョンで保存したファイルを再度送っていただけないでしょうか？

Quick Chat | 咄嗟のひとこと

- We don't have much time.
  私たちには時間がないのです。

key phrases

could you say that again?
もう一度おっしゃっていただけますか？　何か聞き取れなくてもう一度訪ねる時の丁寧な表現。Say that again? Pardon? Excuse me? Sorry? とっさの時にはこのような簡単なワンフレーズでも尋ねられる。

would it be possible to～?
～することは可能ですか？　丁寧なお願いの表現。Would you be able to～?

have/give an opportunity to～
～の機会を得る、～の機会を与える

make a presentation
プレゼンする

could you please～?
～していただけますか？　似た表現で Would you～? もある。Can you～? Do you～? に比べると丁寧だが、その後に please を付けると更に丁寧になる。please の位置は文の最後でも可。

Would you give us a moment, please?
ちょっとお時間いただけますか？

---

vocabulary

contractor　施工業者
most up-to-date drawings　最新版の図面
on site　現場で
tile sample　タイルのサンプル
factory　工場
CAD drawing　CAD 図面
right procedure　正式な手続き
afterwards　後ほど

 OK. We will let you know when we have the material.
了解です。素材が手に入ったらすぐにお知らせします。

71 請求・支払い
Billing/Payment

仕事を受注した側からお金のことを話題にするのは難しいですが、黙っていても相手が手配してくれるかというと、そうとも限りません。後でトラブルにならないためにも早い段階で確認しておくことが大切です。

examples

- The estimation is attached to this email. If you have any queries, please don't hesitate to contact us.
  このメールに見積書を添付します。もし、不明な点などありましたら、気軽にご連絡ください。

- Further to our telephone conversation, please find the invoice attached. Could you please make the payment into our bank account in Japan?
  先程電話でお話ししたように、添付した請求書をご確認ください。私たちの日本の銀行口座へ支払いを御願いできますか？

- Is it possible to visit the site by ourselves?
  私たち自身で現地を訪れることは可能ですか？

- Who will pay our travel and accommodation expenses?
  どなたが交通費と滞在費を払うのでしょうか？

- What did you change from the previous estimation sent the other day?
  先日お送りくださった見積もりからの変更点は？

Quick Chat | 咄嗟のひとこと

Q: Will we be paid for our proposal?
私たちの提案に謝礼は支払われますか？

key phrases

If you have any queries, please don't hesitate to contact us.
もし、不明な点などありましたら、どうぞお気軽にご連絡ください

請求やお願いなど言い切りではなく、もし何か不明な点があれば聞く余地はあるよ、というニュアンス。砕けた感じだと Please let us know もある。

further to our telephone conversation,
電話でお話ししたように。電話やミーティングでの会話を記録としてメールに残す場合の出だしの文章。Further to the minutes of our last meeting, 前回の打ち合わせの議事録にあるように、Further to the last email, 前回のメールにあったように。

please find～
～をご確認ください

make payment into～
～へ支払いをする

Please make the payment for our design fee by the end of next month.
来月末までに設計料を支払ってください。

who will pay～?
どなたが～を支払いますか？

expenses
費用。travel expenses や tranport expenses 交通費。accommodation expenses 滞在費。

---

vocabulary

estimation 見積もり	attached 添付された
query 要望、質問	payment 支払い
hesitate ためらう	bank account 銀行口座
contact 連絡を取る	previous 前回の
invoice 請求書	

 No, but we will pay your traveling expenses.
いえ。しかし、あなたの交通費は支払います。

72 契約
Contract

契約書の締結に至るまでは複雑なやり取りが求められますが、そのためのシンプルなコミュニケーションが不可欠です。

examples

- ▶ Could you please let us know the details of the project contract after our scheme has been adopted?
  私たちの提案が採用された後の契約内容の詳細をお知らせいただけないでしょうか？

- ▶ The participants cannot be involved in the project because it is just an ideas competition.
  これはアイデアコンペであって、応募者は基本設計に関われない。

- ▶ If the project can't be completed due to some fault of your own, will there be a penalty charge?
  もし、あなた側の責任で計画が完成しない場合、違約金は発生しますか？

- ▶ What kind of contracts are there between the project manager, site manager and other team key members?
  プロジェクトマネージャー、現場監督、その他の主要チームメンバーの間ではどのような契約関係にあるのでしょうか？

- ▶ Could you please confirm the contract in relation to the payment at each stage?
  それぞれの段階の支払い契約について確認させてくれませんか？

- ▶ We would like to conclude the agreement before proceeding with the project.
  プロジェクトを進める前に契約の締結をお願い致します。

Quick Chat | 咄嗟のひとこと

- By when should we return this contract?
  いつまでに契約書を返送すればよいですか？

key phrases

be involved in the project
計画に関わる

in relation to〜
〜に関して

at each stage
それぞれの段階で。at every stage すべての段階で、at almost every stage ほとんど全ての段階で、We will pay one by one 一つ一つ支払う。

conclude an agreement
契約を締結する。make a contract や make an agreement.
Would you give us three days before we sign the contract?
契約する前に3日間をくれませんか？

---

vocabulary

contract　契約	what kind of〜?　どのような〜ですか？
scheme　計画	site manager　現場監督
adopt　採用する	confirm　確認する
complete　完成する	conclude　結論付ける、締結する
fault of one's own　〜の責任として	agreement　契約
penalty charge　違約金、罰金	proceed　進める

 Please return it by the end of next month.
来月末までにお願いします。

役割分担の確認
Confirmation of Roles

打合せで各自の役割分担を決めたのならば、自分の役割だけでもかまわないので記録としてメールでもいいので内容を確認しておきたいものです。その際に閲覧者に「何か間違い、不明な点などあれば、気軽に連絡ください。」などと付け加えることも大切です。

examples

▶ Would you please let the contractors know that they will meet the interior designer?
施工業者にはインテリアデザイナーと会うよう伝えてもらえませんか？

▶ How detailed should we make the drawings?
私たちはどこまでの詳細な図面を作成すべきでしょうか？

▶ Can we leave the construction schedule to the site manager?
施工予定表は現場マネージャーに任せていいのでしょうか？

▶ We would like to choose the materials ourselves.
素材の選定を私たちにやらせてください。

▶ We will make arrangements between the furniture builder and painter.
家具職人と塗装屋との段取りを決めましょう。

▶ The plants will be chosen by the landscape designer as a subcontractor.
植栽は外注先のランドスケープデザイナーが選びます。

Quick Chat | 咄嗟のひとこと

Who worked on the fitting detail drawings?
建具詳細図は誰が描いたのですか？

key phrases

how detailed should we~?
どれほど詳細に～すべきですか？
How precise are the drawings expected to be at this stage?
この時期にどれほど正確な図面が求められているのでしょうか？

leave A to B
A を B に任せる
I'll leave it to you.
それを君に任せます。

choose~oneself
～を自身で選定する。自分自身を表現する myself が複数形になると ourselves となる。

make arrangements
段取りを決める、調整する
Could you arrange the site inspection meeting?
現場視察を調整してくれますか？

---

vocabulary

contractor　施工業者、請負業者　　subcontractor　下請け
construction schedule　施工予定　　fitting　建具
arrangements　調整　　　　　　　　detail drawing　詳細図面
furniture builder　家具製作者

 It was the interior designer. The drawings will arrive soon.
インテリアデザイナーです。間もなく届きます。

スケジュールの確認
Confirmation of Schedule

スケジュール管理はコスト管理同様非常に大切なものです。それゆえ、何度でも確認しておくことをお勧めします。また、コミュニケーションの問題があるようならば、ある程度余裕を持ったスケジュールを組み立てるのが鍵です。

examples

- Will you take care of managing the project schedule?
  御社がプロジェクトの進行管理を担当されるのでしょうか？

- Unexpected structures might appear during demolition of the building.
  建物を解体する途中で、予期せぬ構造体が出て来るかもしれません。

- Would you please let us know the approximate schedule for the competition?
  コンペの大まかなスケジュールを教えていただけませんか？

- The project schedule is very tight. Is there room for reconsideration, by any chance?
  計画のスケジュールは非常に厳しいです。もしかして再考の余地はありますか？

- We are absolutely sure not to delay completion. Please start the construction on time.
  私たちは竣工時期を絶対遅らせることはできません。予定通り着工してください。

- We have made the schedule sheet allowing some leeway, to be on the safe side.
  少し余裕を持って工程表を作りました。

Quick Chat ｜咄嗟のひとこと

Q: Is this schedule sheet correct?
この工程表は合っていますか？

key phrases

take care of~
〜を担当する、〜を面倒を見る。look after 〜も類語。
None of them take care of this area!
誰もこの地域を気にしていません。

schedule is very tight
スケジュールがとても厳しい

room for reconsideration
再考の余地

on time
時間通りに、予定通りに。似た表現で on schedule がある。
We are confident about delivering on schedule.
私たちはスケジュール通りに引き渡しをする自信があります。

allow some leeway
余裕をもって

on the safe side
大事をとって、余裕をもって、安全側に立つ
Can we say that we will complete this work by Thursday noon, to be on the safe side?
余裕をもって木曜日正午までにこの仕事を完了させると言っていいですか？

---

vocabulary

manage 管理する	room 余地、余白、余裕
unexpected 予期せぬ	reconsider 再考する
during~ 〜の途中	by any chance もしかして、万一
demolish 解体する	absolutely 絶対に
approximate 大まかな、おおよそ	delay 遅らせる
very tight 非常に厳しい、とてもしんどい	leeway 余裕

 It might be out of date. Do you mind if I double-check?
ちょっと古い情報かも知れません。もう一度確認しても構いませんか？

75 進行管理
Schedule Management

施工現場などでは時間のない中で変更が発生します。相手を信用し、口頭でのやり取りが発生する場合がありますが、のちのトラブルを避けるためにも、正式な資料、図面およびメールなどで記録として残しておくことが大切です。

examples

▶ Which proposal is currently underway?
現在、どちらの案で進んでいますか？

▶ Have you ordered the tiles that we had agreed to use the other day?
先日、使用することに合意したタイルは発注しましたか？

▶ We must finish various bits and pieces.
私たちは様々な雑務を終わらせなけばならない。

▶ When is the delivery date and when will we fix our plan?
納期はいつで、私たちはいつ案を決定しますか？

▶ Could you please amend the red lined area of the drawing?
赤く囲った部分についてやり直してくれないか？

▶ It took more time to work on structure reinforcement than expected.
予想以上に構造補強に時間がかかった。

▶ We will make up for the delay by increasing the number of workers at the finishing stage.
遅れた分は仕上げの段階で作業員を増やし、巻き返します。

🏆 **Quick Chat** │ 咄嗟のひとこと

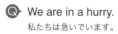 We are in a hurry.
私たちは急いでいます。

key phrases

currently underway
現在進行中の。同じ意味に in progress。
Which area is currently in progress on site?
この現場のどの場所が現在進行中ですか？

red lined area of the drawing
赤線で描かれたエリア

take more time
時間がよりかかる。類似表現に take a time 時間がかかる。take your time ごゆっくりどうぞ。
It might take more time to complete this site.
この現場を完成させるのはより多くの時間がかかるかもしれません。

make up for~
～を挽回する、～を巻き返す
Can you make up for the shortage of builders by employing extra personnel?
施工者が足りないのを追加人員で取り戻せますか？

at the finishing stage
仕上げの段階で

---

vocabulary

currently　現在の
underway　進行中の
order　注文する
agreed to~　～することに同意する
bits and pieces（bits and bobs）
　雑用
delivery date　納期、引き渡し日
fix　決める
amend　修正する、やり直す、修正する
structure reinforcement　構造補強
personnel　人員

 Ok, we will send you the draft first.
オッケー。それではまず下書き送ります。

76 コスト管理
Cost Management

施工段階のコストに関するやり取りはシビアになってきます。ただお願いしたり、拒否するのではなく、プロジェクト完成に向けて歩み寄りを見せるコミュニケーションを取りたいものです。

examples

- ▶ It would be helpful if you could introduce reliable local contractors who can take care of cost management.
  コスト管理の担当ができ、信頼のおける現地の施工業者をご紹介いただけると助かります。

- ▶ If we accept the modifications at this stage, we will exceed the total budget for the project.
  現時点でのこの変更を受け入れたら、計画の総予算を超えることになる。

- ▶ We will do our best even with a low budget.
  たとえ予算が少なくても、私たちはベストを尽くします。

- ▶ Although we might exceed our budget, using better materials will lead to greater durability.
  予算は越えますが、より良い素材を使用することで耐久性は上がります。

- ▶ Could you give us time to arrange a reduction in the cost?
  減額調整をする時間をください。

- ▶ Our client increased the project budget in the end.
  クライアントが最後になって予算を増やしてくれました。

Quick Chat │ 咄嗟のひとこと

- Could you please design this part again?
  ここのデザインはやり直してください。

key phrases

even with a low budget
たとえ低予算でも
The conditions might not be sufficient to design the better architecture, even with a huge budget.
巨額予算があっても、より良い建築を設計する十分条件ではない。

exceed the budget
予算を超える

arrange a reduction in the cost
減額を調整する。cost reduction arrangement 減額調整。
The meeting to arrange cost reductions may be quite intense.
減額調整会議は非常にシビアになるかもしれません。

in the end
最後に。他にも at last、finally などがある。
They finally started working on site.
やっと彼らが現場を開始した。

---

vocabulary

be helpful 〜していただけると助かります	do one's best 最善(ベスト)を尽くす
introduce 紹介する	budget 予算
reliable 信頼できる	exceed 超える
modification 変更、変化、変形	durability 耐久性
	intense 激しい、シビアな

 Ok, but it might cost more.
良いけれど、コストが多くかかるかも。

77 現地調査
Site Survey

限られた時間での効率的な調査をするために、現地調査で起こりうるあらゆる作業を想定して事前に準備をしましょう。

examples

- ▶ Please send us information about the surroundings of the site by mail before visiting.
  現地を訪れる前に周辺情報をメールで送ってください。

- ▶ We will take a tape measure, level and dust-proof camera to the site. Do we need anything else?
  こちらからは巻尺、水平器、防塵カメラを持参します。他に何か必要ですか？

- ▶ The pictures taken during regular site inspections were uploaded into the shared folder.
  定例現場検査で撮影した画像を共有フォルダにアップしておきました。

- ▶ Please bring your own PPE kit, namely a hard-hat, protective gloves, high visibility jacket, safety boots and safety glasses.
  各自PPEキット、すなわちヘルメット、安全グローブ、ジャケット、安全ブーツ、安全ゴーグルの持参をお願いします。

- ▶ Smoking and alcohol are not allowed on the construction site.
  建設現場内での喫煙と飲酒は許されません。

Quick Chat ｜咄嗟のひとこと

- Do we inspect the site even when it rains?
  雨が降っても現地の調査をしますか？

key phrases

information about the surroundings of the site
敷地現場周辺の情報。同様の表現で information around the site がある。

by mail
メールで。mail は正確には郵便になるが、現在 mail と言えば電子メールのこと。郵便では by post という表現がある。
Could you send the paper drawing by post?
紙の図面を郵便で送ってくれませんか？

regular site inspection
定例現場検査。期間には、hourly 毎時間、daily 毎日、weekly 毎週、monthly 毎月、quarterly 3 か月毎、annually 年、などがある。

bring your own PPE kit
自身の PPE キットを持ってくる。PPE とは Personal Protective Equipment の略であり、hard-hat ヘルメット、protective gloves 手袋、high visibility jacket ジャケット、safety boots 安全靴、safety glasses ゴーグル。

---

vocabulary

tape measure　巻き尺
level　水準器
dust-proof camera　防塵カメラ
regular　定期的な

shared folder　共有フォルダー
namely　すなわち
allow　許可する

 Of course.
もちろん。

基本設計
Preliminary Design

基本設計はプロジェクトの初期段階ゆえ大まかな枠組みを決める時期ではあります。それゆえプロジェクトが始まってから無駄なロスを避ける意味でも明確な方向性は示しておきたいところです。

examples

- This preliminary drawing set is no longer valid.
  この基本設計図書一式はもはや有効ではありません。

- There are still many steps before completion of the project following the preliminary design.
  基本設計から建築が完成するのはまだまだ多くのステップがある。

- At this stage, we will check the room layout and circulation using a 1/500 scale model.
  この段階では1/500模型で部屋の配置や動線を確認します。

- Now that the preliminary design is finished, we are currently waiting for the estimation.
  基本設計が終わり、現在見積もりを待っております。

- We incorporated the required functions but cannot decide on the layout.
  必要な機能を盛り込んだが配置が決まりません。

- The preliminary scheme might be changed after arrangements are made for cost reductions.
  減額調整で基本設計が変更になるかもしれません。

Quick Chat | 咄嗟のひとこと

Q: What scale model will we use for the study?
スタディにはどれぐらいの縮尺の模型を使いますか？

key phrases

preliminary design
基本設計。construction design 実施設計。

1/500 scale model
1/500 模型。1/500 の読み方は one to five hundred。〜分の 1 は one to〜 となる。例えば 1/1250 ならば one to one thousand, two hundred and fifty もしくは one to twelve fifty（1250 を 12 と 50 に分けて呼ぶ）。

now that〜
〜だから、〜する以上は

incorporate the required functions
要求された機能を盛り込む

---

vocabulary

drawing set　図面一式	at this stage　この段階で
no longer valid　もはや有効でない	1/500 scale model　1/500 模型
completion　完成	currently　現在
preliminary design　基本設計	

 I think 1/1000 (one to one thousand) would be enough.
1/1000 で十分だと思います。

79 見積もり
Estimation/Quotation

見積もりなどお金の絡んだやり取りには交渉力が求められます。なるべく曖昧な表現は避けましょう。そして少しでも不明な点があれば、何度でも確認すべきですし、メールや文面などで記録として取っておくと後々トラブルに合いません。

examples

▶ Would it be possible to add currency exchange rates on the excel sheet for clarification?
正確を期すためにエクセルシートに為替レートを加えることは可能ですか？

▶ Please find an enclosed estimation for your information.
ご参考までに見積書を同封いたしますので、ご査収ください。

▶ Is it possible to have competitive quotations?
相見積もりを取らせていただくことは可能ですか？

▶ Don't you think this estimation is slightly vague?
この見積もりは少々甘いと思いませんか？

▶ The estimation is ten million yen more than anticipated.
見積もりが予想より1000万円オーバーしてしまいました。

▶ Going over the quotation by this much is still within our expectations. We will be able to make adjustments later.
このぐらいの見積もりオーバーはまだ私たちの想定内です。今後調整します。

Quick Chat | 咄嗟のひとこと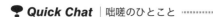

Q: Does this price include the consumption tax?
その値段に消費税は含まれていますか？

key phrases

for clarification
正確を期すため。何かをお願いする際の念押しに使える。Just for clarification となると「ホントに些細なことなんだけれど…」というニュアンスになる。

please find an enclosed～
同封した～をご査収ください。メール添付の場合は Please find an attached quotation となる。

for your information
報告として。情報を伝えたい相手だけでなくクライアントや上司への報告の際に使う。メールで言うところの CC。文書などでは F.Y.I の略語となる。

have competitive quotations
相見積もりを取る

going over the quotation
見積もりをオーバーする。同じ意味に exceed the estimation。
This change exceeds the original quotation.
この変更は当初の見積もりを超えます。

within expectations
想定内の。unexpected 想定外の。

make adjustments
調整する

---

vocabulary

add 加える	competitive quotation 相見積もり
currency exchange rate 為替レート	vague 曖昧な
clarification 説明、明確さ	more than anticipated 予想以上に
enclose 同封する	by this much この程度の
estimation 見積もり	

 Yes, the consumption tax is 20% in this country.
はい、この国の消費税は 20 パーセントです。

実施設計
Construction Design

実施図面になると基本設計とは違い、より多くの専門用語が登場してきます。その上、そのプロジェクトや現場だけで通じる略語などが出てきます。その際には略語一覧を見つける（もしくは作成する）のが重要です。

examples

- We will start working on the construction drawings after receiving the estimation from the contractors.
  施工業者からの見積もりが取れた後に実施図面の作成を始めます。

- The drawings for the contractor's tender should be accurate in order to estimate the right cost.
  正しい金額を出すために施工入札のための図面は正確を期さなければならない。

- We will confirm the specific location of this tree on site.
  この樹木の正確な場所は現場で確認します。

- Would you please issue a bar chart of the construction schedule?
  施工工程表の棒グラフ（横線工程表）の発行をお願いできますか？

- Please make sure to circulate the updated drawings among all contractors at the construction site.
  更新された図面が工事現場の全作業員にきちんと行き渡るようにしてください。

- Please issue the abbreviation list on the first page.
  短縮語一覧をまず図面の一番最初に添付してください。

Quick Chat | 咄嗟のひとこと

What does this symbol mean on this drawing?
この図面内のこの記号は何を意味するの？

key phrases

be accurate
正確を期す。正確を期して for accuracy。類語として precise、exact などがある。

estimate the right cost
正しい金額を見積もる

confirm on site
現場で確認する。類例として図面上では T.B.C on site（To Be Confirmed on site の略。現場にて確認のこと）と表記される。確認するには double-check〔動詞〕もある。

We will double-check the drawing before dispatch.
発送する前に図面を再確認しましょう

make sure to〜
必ず〜するようにする

abbreviation list
略語リスト。BOH、AOB、EP、HP、WP など日常業務には多くの略語が飛び交う。業界全体で共通となっている略語はあるが、プロジェクト独自の略語やチームメンバーのイニシャルが入ると把握できないため、リストを見つけるなりして全体像を把握しておきたい。

---

vocabulary

contractor's tender　施工入札	bar chart　棒グラフ（横線工程表）
accurate　正確な	circulate among〜　〜に回覧する
estimate　予想する	updated　更新された、最新版の
right　正しい	abbreviation list　略語リスト
specific　特別な	

 Have you checked the symbol list?
記号一覧見ました？

81 施工現場
Construction Site

施工現場は危険を伴う場所なので、そのコミュニケーションには正しい英語はもちろんのこと、挨拶をする、目を見て話すなどの基本的な振る舞いが求められます。その振る舞いなしに正しい英語を使えても現場の作業員には伝わりません。

examples

- Please conduct a geological survey of the site to research for piling.
  杭打ちの検討のために地質調査をお願いします。

- The site engineers are awaiting further instructions from you.
  現場のエンジニアたちはあなたからのさらなる指示を待っています。

- Please inform all contractors on site to keep it tidy at all times.
  現場の全作業員にいつもきちんと整理するように周知してください。

- Please hold the ladder with both hands.
  はしごは両手でつかんで利用してください。

- The large machinery will be brought onto the site to excavate.
  大きな切削機器が工事現場に運び込まれます。

- The horizontal and vertical level of the existing building should be reconfirmed.
  既存建物の水平垂直が取れているか再確認しなければならない。

Quick Chat | 咄嗟のひとこと

Q: How long does it take for concrete to dry?
コンクリートが乾くまでどれくらいかかりますか？

key phrases

geological survey
地質調査。似た表現で geological research や geological examination などがある。

keep~tidy
～を整理する。似た表現に clean up や organize や sort out などがある。
Please clean up at the end of the day before you go.
1日が終わったら整理してから帰ってください。

bring onto~
～へ運び込む。似た表現に carry in などがある。運ぶには convey などがある。
Please convey the gravel to the site.
砂利を現場まで運んでください。

---

vocabulary

conduct　行う	ladder　はしご
piling　杭	with both hands　両手で
site engineer　現場のエンジニア	machinery　機械
await　待つ	bring　持ってくる、運び込む
further　さらなる	excavate　切削する
instructions　指示	horizontal and vertical　水平垂直
at all times　いつも	reconfirm　再確認

Ⓐ About five days in this season.
　この季節なら約5日間です。

納まりの施工
Construction Details

阿吽の呼吸がない海外の施工現場では、おかしなところがあっても図面通りに施工されることがあります。正確な数値などを記載することはもちろんのこと、常に密なコミュニケーションを取り、確認を取りたいものです。

examples

- The material for the balcony handrails was decided to fit with the surroundings.
  周辺環境に合わせてバルコニーの手すりの材質を決めました。

- Please double-check the size of the stair tread and riser to match the regulations.
  法規に従っているか、階段の踏面と蹴上のサイズを今一度確認ください。

- Simply said, the edges of the plaster wall are concealed with the door architraves.
  簡単に言うと、漆喰壁の端はドア額縁の中に隠れています。

- By when do I have to decide the window size?
  いつまでに窓のサイズを決めなければなりませんか？

- Let's research with an actual 1:1 scale mockup on site.
  現場で原寸1:1のモックアップで検証しましょう。

- We would like to talk about the details.
  納まりについて少しお話しさせてください。

Quick Chat | 咄嗟のひとこと

Q: Would it be possible for you to send photos of the site?
現場写真を送ってもらえますか？

key phrases

to fit with the surroundings
周辺に合わせて

stair tread and riser
階段の踏面と蹴上。階段の詳細として nosing 段鼻、landing 踊り場、balustrade 手すり、door architraves ドアの額縁、door frame ドア枠、hinge 蝶番、door leaf 扉、kick plate 蹴板、 door handle 取っ手、door lock 錠前。

match the regulations
法規に従って

simply said
簡単に言うと

with an actual 1:1 scale mock-up
原寸 1:1 のモックアップで

would like to talk about~
~について話をしたい

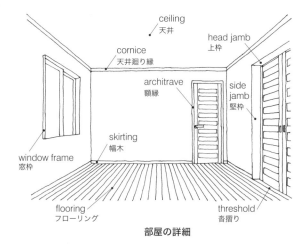

部屋の詳細

- ceiling 天井
- cornice 天井廻り縁
- head jamb 上枠
- architrave 額縁
- side jamb 堅枠
- skirting 幅木
- window frame 窓枠
- flooring フローリング
- threshold 沓摺り

---

vocabulary

balcony	バルコニー	edge	際、端
handrail	手すり	plaster	しっくい、石こう
double-check	再チェック	door architraves	ドア枠
regulation	法規	by when	いつまでに
simply said	簡単に言うと	actual	原寸
concealed	隠れた		

 Ok, which particular area do you need photos of?
了解です。特にどの場所の写真が必要ですか？

納まりの表現
Expressions about Details

日本人の求める建築詳細の水準に対して、現地の施工技術がその水準に追いつかないかも知れませんが、言語だけでなく図面、写真などあらゆる手段を講じて少しでも近づける努力したいものです。

examples

▶ Please install the stone tiles with less than a 3mm gap to avoid fingers getting trapped.
指が入るのを避けるため石のタイルは3mm以下の隙間で設置してください。

▶ The wooden floor parquets are laid with tolerance at the edge of the room to allow for expansion.
木ブロック床材は伸縮性を考慮し、部屋外周部に十分な遊びを取って敷かれている。

▶ Please cut the timber with a 45-degree angle to hide the ends.
小口が出ないように木材は45度の角度で切り出してください。

▶ Please finish the details so that the tread hides the end of the riser.
踏面材が蹴上材に勝つ（隠す）よう詳細を処理してください。

▶ Please make the edges safe to avoid causing harm to users.
利用者が怪我するのを避けるよう角を安全に処理してください。

🍷 Quick Chat ｜咄嗟のひとこと

Q We haven't constructed this type of detailed work before.
このような詳細を以前施工したことありません。

key phrases

install
設置する

Please install downlights every 2m.
2m 毎にダウンライトを設置してください。

avoid A ~ ing
A が〜するのを避ける。公共建築のように様々な利用者を想定する場合、finger trap（指が挟まる場所）が生まれないように気を付けましょう。

A 7mm gap would become a finger trap.
7mm の隙間は指が挟まるかもしれません。

be laid with tolerance
遊びをとって敷かれる、設置される。tolerance 許容誤差。

allow for expansion
伸縮性を考慮する。clearance や spare space など施工精度の違いや気象条件による伸縮性を考慮して余裕を持たせた詳細を指示します。

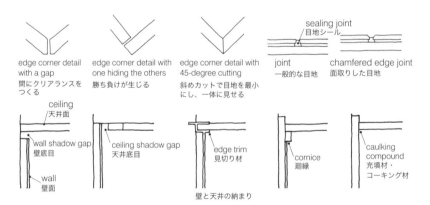

納まりやとりあいを伝える

---

vocabulary

stone tile	石タイル	hide the ends	末端を隠す
gap	隙間	edge	角、端
trapped	挟まった	cause	もたらす、引き起こす
parquet	木ブロック床材	harm	傷つける
tolerance	許容誤差、遊び	joint	とりあい
expansion	伸縮性		

 No worries, I will send you the detail drawings by fax in five minutes.
大丈夫です。5 分以内にファックスで詳細図面を送ります。

竣工・引き渡し
Completion/Delivery

プロジェクトが完成しました。関係者とは良いことも悪いことも共有したに違いありません。しかし、世界を舞台にしたとしても建築業界は狭い。次の出会いでも気持ちよく再会できるように、ねぎらいやお祝いの言葉をかけたいものです。

examples

- We would like to join the completion inspection.
  完了検査の際には参加したいです。

- We were able to complete this project thanks to such a wonderful team. Thank you very much.
  素晴らしいチームのお陰でプロジェクトは完成しました。ありがとうございました。

- You coordinated and managed between clients very well.
  あなたは施主と私たちの間で調整と管理をよくしてくれました。

- The project is a success! We are looking forward to working with you next time.
  プロジェクトは成功しました。次回も是非ご一緒できるのを楽しみにしております。

- We are delighted to open this facility. Congratulations!
  弊社もこの施設がオープンしたことを嬉しく思います。おめでとうございます。

- We have accomplished the project and look forward to working together with you again.
  私たちはプロジェクトは終えましたが、再びご一緒できることを楽しみにしております。

Quick Chat | 咄嗟のひとこと

 We made it!
私たちはよくやった！

key phrases

complete
完成する。似た表現では accomplish、achieve、finish、terminate など。
This project will terminate in a few days.
この計画はあと数日で終わりを迎えます。

thanks to such a wonderful team
素晴らしいチームのおかげで

look forward to~
～することを楽しみにしている。to の後には名詞。
We look forward to the next project in the near future.
私たちは近々、次のプロジェクトを楽しみにしております。

work together with~
～と一緒に働く。似た表現に collaborate with~ や team up with~、partner with~ など。
Let's team up together for another competition!
他のコンペティションで皆さんとチームを組みましょう。

---

vocabulary

completion　完成、竣工	success　成功
inspection　検査、調査	be delighted　嬉しい
wonderful　素晴らしい	congratulations　おめでとう
coordinate　調整する	accomplish　完成する、達成する
manage　管理する	

 Yes, we are a brilliant team.
はい、私たちは本当にいいチームだった。

撮影・画像処理
Photo Shoot/Image Processing

SNSやウェブメディア全盛の現代、建築写真の伝達力、伝播力は絶大です。写真家の腕前を信頼する一方、その建築の見せどころを一番よく知っているのは設計者自身でもあります。良いアングルを切り取れるよう、的確な指示を出しましょう。

examples

- We are looking for a photographer to shoot a Japanese style interior.
  和風内装を撮影してくれるカメラマンを探しています。

- I am not sure that there is enough space for a tripod.
  三脚を設置するための十分な場所があるかわかりません。

- Please take photos without people's reflections in the glass.
  ガラスに人が映らないように撮ってください。

- What would be the best time for a photo shoot on site?
  現地では何時が最適な撮影時間でしょうか？

- What kind of weather is good for an interior photo shoot?
  どのような天気が、インテリア撮影に向いていますか？

- Is it possible to change the brightness using graphics software afterwards?
  後ほど、グラフィックソフトを使って明度を変更することは可能ですか？

Quick Chat | 咄嗟のひとこと

- We would like you to take pictures on a sunny day.
  晴れの日に撮影してほしい。

key phrases

space for a tripod
三脚用のスペース。撮影機材には他に lighting equipment 照明設備、reflector 反射板、stepladder 脚立など。

take a photo
写真を撮る。写真は picture や photograph ともいう。take a movie 動画を撮影する。

without reflections in the glass
ガラスに映り込まないで

what would be the best time for～?
～に最適の時間はいつですか？ 天候、日照、屋内、屋外で撮影にベストな時間帯が違ってくるので、あらかじめ確認しておきたい。

what kind of～?
どんな～ですか？
What kind of photo are you looking for?
どんなお写真をお探しですか？

be good for～
～に向いている、適している

---

vocabulary

look for ～ /search for～ ～を探す	resolution 解像度
photographer 写真家	hue 色相
shoot 写真を撮る	chroma 彩度
tripod 三脚	brightness 明度
reflection 反射	aspect ratio/horizontal to vertical ratio 縦横比
photo shoot 写真撮影	

 It might be difficult in this season, but we will do our best.
この季節は難しいけれど、ベストは尽くします。

コラム③

会議には 70％の気持ちで臨む（事前準備は 120％で）

　建設施工現場では常に問題が噴出し、監理建築士の気の休まる時はありません。また建築士が定例会議でつるし上げを食らうのは、どうやら日本の建設現場だけではないようです。私自身、地下鉄駅の現場監理を担当した定例会議の帰り道、現場近くの国際特急ユーロスターの発着駅からそのままユーロスターに乗ってヨーロッパ大陸に逃げてしまいたいと思ったのは一度や二度ではありません。

　建築士が現場の人たちから煙たがられるのは世界共通のようです。それゆえ、ごまかさず毎週の定例会議の前は 120％の準備をするようにしていました。会議の準備を入念にすれば問題は既に解決していたり、それほど深刻ではないことに気付くこともありました。また、他の参加者からどんな指摘が出てくるか、シュミレーションもできます。議題や確認事項と共に解決策までを会議参加者に前もって送ってしまえば、当日の会議は議論するよりもそれらについて YES か NO の承認を取る場にすることができます。

　また、会議が終わったら、自分の担当区分だけでも議事録メモにして提出してしまうのも、次回会議に向けた究極の事前準備となり得ます。参加者全員に「For your information（F.Y.I. ご参考までに）」と記して回覧し、何か間違いや不足があれば（英語の間違いを含め！）、チェックしてもらえるかもしれません。

　現場は想定外の出来事が必ず起こります。それを慣れない言語で対応するのですから、余裕をもってあらゆる事態を想定し準備をしておくのが理想です。そうすれば、リラックスした 70％の気持ちで会議に臨め、新たな問題に直面しても、集中して取り組むことができるはずです。

地下鉄駅改修工事現場での風景。建設現場ではシンプルなコミュニケーションが求められます。

〈会議議事録のサンプル〉

TOKYO CENTRAL STATION TICKET HALL [←プロジェクト名]
ARCHITECTURAL CO-ORDINATION MEETING [←ミーティング名]
MEETING MINUTES & ACTION NOTES (議事録と実施担当者記録)

Date (日付)	Monday 6th September 2016
Location (場所)	KZYA meeting room- KZYA office
Attendees (参加者)	Neil Harding, NH [←略称], NH Consultants Ltd [←所属先] Peter Weaver, PW, PW Engineering Partners Kazuya Yamazaki, KY, KZY Architects
Apologies (欠席者)	Steve Butler(KZYA), Mathew Frost(PWE), Lea Yates(NHC), Bob Morrison(KZYA), Graham Allies(PWE)
Distribution (議事録配布者)	those present plus (参加者＋) Chris Weaver, Yoko Sanchez

Item (項目)	Minute (議事録)	Action (実施担当者)
1	CNTRL new gate [←具体的な議題]	
1.1	KY to confirm heights of gates. TBC on next site visit.	KY
1.2	PW noted that the wall construction needs to achieve 1-hour fire rating.	PW
1.3	…	
2	Review of previous Actions (from meeting 08/08/16) (前回会議以降の実施内容レビュー)	
2.1	Existing gate issue will be discussed in Workshop on 12/08.	All
2.2	…	
3	Matters arising (新しい課題)	
3.1	Further back-up information on the new steel gate is requested. KY will confirm what spec is required.	KY
3.2	…	
4	Planned workshops (今後のワークショップの予定)	
4.1	Kiosk manager's workshop- Wednesday at 2pm, KZYA office	PW&SB
4.2	Future gate workshops- Friday at 2pm, KZYA office	PW&KY
5	Next meeting (次回会議)	
5.1	Monday 20th September at 2pm, in KZYA office.	All

Meeting minutes produced by: Kazuya Yamazaki(KZYA) [←議事録作成者名]

おわりに

異なる言語を手に入れることは、異なる考え方を手に入れること

　異なる言語を手に入れるということはどのようなことなのでしょうか。
　母国語ではない外国語を身に着ける過程には「自分が本当に言いたいことは何か」を問い直す瞬間や、日本語でコミュニケーションしているときには気付かなかったことを発見します。同様に外国語を身に着けることでコミュニケーションできる相手の数も増えます。私自身、渡英前には予想しなかった考え方、働き方、そして生き方が世界にあると気付かされました。
　実務経験も英語能力もほとんどない中で渡英した当時、もし本書のようなコンセプトの本があったら、私の英国での英語力や仕事の経歴は違ったものになっていたのではないかと思います。そのような一人の日本人が海外の建築現場で肌で感じた疑問やそこから身に着いたコミュニケーションスキルを本書には多く盛り込みました。
　仕事現場のシーンを想定した本書は学生の読者にとっては少しイメージしづらかったかもしれません。しかし、お金を払って生活する海外留学と、お金をもらって生活する海外就労では世界の見え方が180度変わります。英語が通じなければクビになるという緊張感の中で働くことに是非チャレンジしてみてください。職場のリアルな様子はイギリス人の働き方について述べた拙著『イギリス人の、割り切ってシンプルな働き方』(KADOKAWA) に詳しく綴ったので、実際に海外の事務所で働く機会や協働する時には本書と一緒

に参照してみてください。接し方や考え方のヒントになるはずです。

本書の始まりは「海外で働く日本の建築業界の方に向けた本を作りませんか？」という学芸出版社・編集室長である井口夏実さんからのメールでした。作業は建築実務の現場を思い浮かべながら日本文を書き出し、そこに英文を加えるという、気の遠くなるものでした。しかし、敏腕編集長の繊細な手綱さばきと大胆な校正によって本書は完成しました。お礼申し上げます。

はじめにでも書いたとおり、やはり外国語を身に着けるには建築の現場でのコミュニケーションを通して嫌な思い、悔しい思い、そして冷や汗をかくのが一番の近道になるはずです。世界を相手に働く日本人建築士たちにとって本書がその役に立つのならば、著者としてこれほどの喜びはありません。

ロンドン五輪会場での筆者後姿。新しい言語を手に入れることで日本をソトから客観的に見られます。

2016年8月　山嵜一也

英語索引

■ A

abbreviation list ……………173
absolutely ……………161
absorb ……………75
absorb light ……………75
accessible ……………129
accomplish ……………181
accurate ……………173
acoustic insulation ……………111
acoustic insulation sheet ………111
acoustics ……………111
actual ……………177
activity ……………92
add ……………171
additional ……………67
adequate ……………79, 97
adjacent ……………17
adjacent house ……………11
adjustment ……………91, 171
administrative role ……………41
adopt ……………51, 157
advertisement ……………45
advertising panel ……………31
affordability ……………37
affordable price ……………29
afraid that ……………139
after completion ……………127
afterwards ……………153
against ……………51, 83, 143
agenda ……………139
agree ……………63
agree that ……………63
agreed to ……………163
agreement ……………157
aid concentration ……………93
aim ……………51
air conditioning ……………23
air environment ……………107
air flow ……………37
air pollution ……………43
air-conditioning ……………63
align with ……………29
aligned with ……………67
allow ……………167
allow for ……………55, 123, 179
allow some leeway ……………161
allowing easy access ………47
along ……………31, 57
alternative ……………117
alternatively ……………151
although ……………57, 125
ambiguous ……………27, 70, 71

amend ……………163
amidst ……………59
among ……………131
amount ……………37, 39
amount of ……………123
analyze ……………119, 125
another ……………117
answer questions ……………135
anticipation ……………57
appendix ……………119
application ……………135, 143
apply to ……………140, 141
approach ……………24, 25
approach A via B ……………25
appropriate ……………107, 111
approve ……………95, 97
approximate ……………161
architrave ……………177
architectural environment ……110
architectural standards law ……23
around ……………103
arrange ……………165
arrange in ……………143
arrangements ……………159
artificial leaves ……………129
asking questions ……………134
as if ……………87
as much as ……………133
as outlined below ……………117
as~as possible ……………73
as well ……………47
Asian atmosphere ……………21
aspect ……………125
assemblage ……………49
assemblage on site ……………49
at all times ……………175
at each stage ……………157
at the actual site ……………119
at the bottom of a mountain ……35
at the end of ……………39
at the finishing stage ……………163
at the moment ……………125
at the rear ……………13
at the same time ……………43, 63
at this stage ……………169
atmosphere ……………83
atrium ……………23, 129
attached ……………155
attachment ……………151
attention ……………117
attract customers ……………33
auditorium ……………47, 111

authentic ……………85
auto-locking system ……………25, 109
autoclaved lightweight concrete panel ……………89
avoid ……………29, 61, 179
avoiding a quick response ……136
await ……………175

■ B

back garden ……………57
background ……………115
back of house ……………59, 123
balcony ……………61, 177
balustrade ……………55, 89
bamboo forest ……………21
bank account ……………155
bar chart ……………173
bare skeleton ……………45
barrier-free ……………41
based on ……………17, 119
basement ……………67
bathroom ……………55, 57
bay windows ……………65
beam ……………99
beauty ……………33
because ……………11, 35
become an ambiguous place ……27
belonging ……………39
bench ……………23
beneath ……………103
benefit ……………133
benefits and losses ……………133
beside ……………47
best suited ……………139
between A and B ……………63
bicycle parking space ……………17
billing ……………154
bind ……………143
binding ……………143
bits and pieces(bits and bobs) …163
blank space ……………143
blind ……………87
block the view ……………17
blockwork ……………111
book ……………151
booth ……………69
boundary ……………57
brace ……………99
brace structure ……………101
brand new building ……………133
brickwork ……………83
brief ……………115, 141

brief summary ·············143	cladded ················81	concentrate ···············93
bright ················79	cladding ················91	concept ················119
brighter ···············133	cladding exterior ·········88	concept of ···············27
brightness···········74, 78	clarification ············171	conclude ···········115, 157
brilliant ···············125	clarify ················71	conclude an agreement ·······157
bring ··········131, 167, 175	claw feet ···············83	concluding business ········138
bring onto ·············175	clean up···············123	conclusion···············139
budget ··········49, 67, 165	clear················41	concrete base ············111
buffer zone ···············27	clear-lacquered ············91	concrete slab············111
builder ················159	clearly ············59, 151	condition ······32, 73, 91, 95, 143
building ··········15, 23, 105	cliff edge ··············69	condominium apartment ·······37
building coverage ratio ······95	climate················65	conduct ················175
building manager's office ·······109	close ················68	conduit ················103
building outline ···········31	closet ················57	confirm ············150, 157, 173
building paper ············111	close to ···············69	confirm on site ············173
built to···············37	co-worker ··············93	confirm whether ············141
business ··············53	coast ·················13	confirmation ········158, 160, 171
business plan ············127	collaborate··············141	confirming document ········150
bustle ················15	collaboration ·············141	congested ···············59
by any chance ············161	collaborator ··············97	congestion ···············33
by combining ············105	color ··········55, 74, 75	congratulations ············181
by email attachment·········143	column···············99	connect ···········11, 63
by mail ···············167	combat ···············109	connection ···············69
by this much ············171	come to one's mind ·········125	consider ·········15, 51, 63
by when ···············177	comfort ················49	consideration ·······23, 87, 105
	comfortable ··············33	construction cost ·············49
■ C	comment ···············147	construction design ············172
CAD drawing ············153	commercial ··············95	construction details ···········176
carefully laid out ···········129	commercial building ······19, 44, 46	construction law ··········96
carpet ················111	commercial district ··········95	construction method ···49, 100, 101
casement windows··········65	commercialize············43	construction schedule ·······159
cater ················45	communal ··············73	construction site ··········174
caulking compound ·········179	communal facility ··········127	consumption behavior ·········47
cause ················179	communal space ···········25	contact ················155
ceiling ···71, 79, 91, 111, 129, 177, 179	community ··········17, 69	continually ···············87
ceiling panel ··············91	community center ··········17	contract···············156, 157
ceiling shadow gap ·········179	commuter ···········41, 59	contractor ···········153, 159
center on···············33	compact ···············121	contractor's tender ·········173
challenging ···············131	comparing ···············120	contrarily················49
chamfer ················29	comparison ········33, 121	contrast ···········85, 121
chamfered edge joint ········179	compare···············120	contrast with ·············85
cheerful atmosphere ·········33	competition ·············141	conventional ··············131
cherry tree ···············21	competitive quotation ········171	conversation ··············155
children's room ············57	complete ·········157, 181	convey·················21
choose~oneself ············159	completion ······169, 180, 181	coordinate ··············181
chroma ················74	complex ·········69, 125	cope ·················65
circular ················31	complexity ···············33	cope with ···············65
circulate A to B ···········137	comply with ··············97	cork flooring ···············91
circulate among ···········173	comprehensive ············23	corner ·················29
circulation ·······45, 58, 59, 129	comprehensive design system	cornice ············177, 179
citizen ················41	·················23, 95	corridor ···········31, 57, 71
cityscape ··············147	compression ··············99	cost ···49, 121, 123, 127, 131, 165, 173
clad ·················81	comtemporary life ·········83	
	concealed ·············177	cost effectiveness ··········45

cost management ··············164	despite ··································61	eave ·······························17, 101
cost more ··························49	detail drawing ·····················159	echo ································111
could you please~? ···············153	detailed information ········137, 141	eco-friendly ·························51
country house ······················35	difference ·····························37	ecological ························50
courier ································151	different ······················121, 145	edge ···························177, 179
courteously ·······················147	direct sunlight ·····················51	edge corner detail with a gap ···179
courtyard ·······················11, 57	directly ·································129	edge corner detail with one hiding
cover with······················17, 73	disabled parking space ············17	the others ·····················179
covered ·····························73	disconnect A from B ·············75	edge corner detail with 45-degree
create a flow ······················29	disconnected ·······················75	cutting ·······························179
create an air-flow ··················55	discussion ····························93	edge trim ·····················91, 179
create atmosphere ···················21	discussion among ··················93	edit ·································145
creating presentation data ······144	disorder ································33	effect ·····················25, 51, 81
creating proposal document ···142	distinguishing ····················119	effectiveness ······················49
creative process ··················145	district·································97	efficiency ··························39
critical ·······························127	disturbing ····························75	elderly ································93
critical point ······················127	divide into ···························29	electrical cable tube ·············103
crossing ······························23	do one's best·······················165	electrical room ····················129
currency exchange rate ·········171	do you mind if~? ················135	electricity pole ·················15, 61
current ·······························125	document ·····················137, 150	elevation ·····························29
current changes ··················133	dome structure·····················101	eligible to ························141
current plan ·······················127	door architraves ··················177	eliminate ····························49
currently ·····················163, 169	dot-dash line ·······················11	emerge ·······························93
currently underway ·············163	dotted ·································33	emerge out of ······················93
curved ·······························31	dotted around ······················33	emergency staircase ···········109
customer··························41, 117	dotted with ··························39	emphasize ···················71, 121
cycle path ······················23, 43	double-check·······················177	emphasizing ·······················120
	double hung windows ············65	empty house ·······················53
■ D	double sided ·······················135	enclose ·······························171
damp-proof layer ················111	downtown district ···············147	enclosed ·····················93, 171
damp-proof membrane ········111	drain pipe ··························103	endure ································77
dark ·································139	drainage ······························17	enhance ······························45
daylight ······························63	draughts ····························107	enough ································63
dead angle························109	drain pipe ··························101	enter ·································141
define ································95	drawing ····················121, 143, 163	entrance ······················17, 24, 57
defined by ···························95	drawing scale ·····················151	entry to a competition ··········140
delay ·································161	drawing set ························169	enveloped with ···················105
delighted ·····························181	dry area ·······························17	environment·····················12, 13
delighted to ·······················147	dry landscape garden ·············19	era ····································41
delivery······························180	drying area ··························57	erect ··························17, 105
delivery date·······················163	duct ·································103	escape route ························97
deliveryman ·······················109	due to ·································95	estimate ·····························173
demolish ·······················99, 161	durability ·····························165	estimation·············155, 170, 171
demonstrate ···················33, 81	durable ·······························85	evacuation ··························59
dense ·································75	during ·································161	evacuation route·················59
dense area ·····················11, 105	dust-proof camera ···············167	even if ································53
dense space ·······················75		even though ······················141
depth ·································67	■ E	even with ··························165
describe ······························75	e.g. ····································21	evergreen tree ·····················21
describe A as B ·····················75	e-book ································41	examine ······················53, 125
design ·······························147	earthquake resistance ············99	examine to what extent············53
design to give views of ··········13	earthquake-proof ·············49, 53	excavate ····························175
design with consideration for ···111	easier ·································65	exceed································95, 165
designed to go at ··················47	easy ·································129	exceed the budget ··············165

existing ··67	fingerprint-proof ·····················91	front road ································11, 95
existing building ······················49	finish ·····························19, 89, 91	function ··································54, 169
expansion ·····························179	finish soon·······························139	furniture ··86
expect ··································123	finishing material ··················49	furniture builder ··················159
expectation ····················81, 171	fire extinguisher ··················103	furniture layout ·····················87
expenses ·······························155	fireproof·································105	further····························41, 175
experience ·····························141	fire protection ·····················104	further to our telephone conversa-
explain ···································115	fire resistance ······················104	tion ·····································155
explaining advantages and disad-	fire separation wall ··············105	
vantages ·····························132	fire-rated ·······························105	■ G
explaining maintenance arrange-	fire-rated foam ·····················103	gable roof ·······························101
ments ·································128	fire-resistant ··························105	gain ···························27, 63, 127
explaining the cost ···············126	firm ·······································121	gain more attention from·········117
explore ···························13, 119	first of all ·······················49, 115	galvalume steel plate ···············89
explore the concept ···············119	first priority ····························35	gap·································103, 179
exposed concrete ············89, 101	fishing industry ·······················13	gap between A and B ··········103
expression ································70	fit ···125	garden ·························18, 19, 57
expressions about details ······178	fit in···11	gather ·······························63, 93
expressions for press release ···146	fit the requirements···············125	gathering space ·······················41
extent ····································125	fitting ·····································159	generous use of ·······················21
extension ·································53	fix ···163	gentle connection ···················71
exterior ····································27	fixed shelf ·······························87	genuine ····································85
external····························11, 27	fixed windows··························65	geological survey ··················175
external building skin ···········107	flat roof ·································101	get back to ·····························137
external envelope ····················69	floating screed ·······················111	give a brief ·····························115
external work ···························16	floor area ratio ·······27, 39, 95, 127	give a luxurious feel ···············91
extra care ······························101	floor finish······························111	give a moment ······················137
extremely ································79	flooring ··································177	give a presentation ···············115
eye-level ··································69	floor tile ································111	give a warm feeling ················71
	flourescent light ······················79	give an opportunity to ··········153
■ F	flow ···59	give comments ·······················147
facade ·······························15, 28	flow angle ······························103	give consideration to ············105
face ··109	flower bed ································17	give importance to··················37
facilitate·································129	flower petal·····························21	giving examples ······················118
facing pages ···························143	following ·······························117	giving reasons ·························118
factory·····························49, 153	for citizens ·······························41	glass ··45
fake ···85	for clarification ······················171	going over the quotation ·······171
family apartment ·····················37	for maintenance ···········21, 65, 89	good for·································183
fan ···107	for security ······························17	government office ···················41
farming village ························13	for security reasons ···············109	grade ··72
fault ·······································157	for severe climate ···················65	gradient regulation················97
fault of one's own ··················157	for the following reason ·······117	granite stone ···························17
feasible ··································125	for these reasons ···················119	gravel ································17, 19
feasibility ·······························124	for universal design ···············55	gravel path ·······························25
feature ·····································31	for visual connection ··············69	green wall ·······························129
feel oppressive ·························27	for your infomation ···············171	grid line ···································29
feel uncomfortable ················133	form ···30	grid number ···························151
feeling ··························17, 29, 71	formed by ································31	groove ·······························17, 29
fence ·······································17	frame structure ·····················101	grooved ····································89
fiber reinforced plastic (FRP) ···91	freestanding wall ····················25	guest room ·······························57
filter··93	from floor to ceiling ·········35, 63	gutter ·······························29, 101
filtered sunlight ·······················21	from several aspects ············125	
final ·······································145	from the perspective of ····43, 99	■ H
fingerprint ·······························91	front garden ····························57	hammer ··································91

handing over ······150	image processing ······182	issuer······151
handrail······55, 87, 177	imaginary water flow ······19	it is difficult to ······133
hanger ······91	immediately ······59	it is hard to ······15, 107
hard water ······91	importance ······37	it is hard for A to B ······59
harf-Japanese and harf-Western ······83	important ······127	it would be appreciated if ······147
harm ······179	improve ······43	
harmonize with ······13	in a poor condition ······73	■ J
have an opportunity to······153	in accordance with ······23, 53	Japanese construction law······94
have competitive quotations ···171	in collaboration with ······141	Japanese paper ······57
have presence······67	in comparison to ······33, 121	Japanese style······83
have something to share ······139	in conclusion ······139	joint ······179
have the effect of ······25	in front of ······15	
have you checked~? ······151	in other words ······121	■ K
head jamb ······177	in relation to ······91, 157	keep~low ······67
heat ······106	in terms of ······37	keep~tidy······175
heat insulation ······107	in the center of ······57	key factor ······37
heat-proof ······49	in the end ······165	kindergarten ······77
hedge ······17	in various situations ······57	kitchen ······57, 67
height ······67, 97	in~years ······123	
height limit ······37, 97	include ······131	■ L
height of the beam ······99	inclusion of ······41	ladder ······175
height restriction ······95	income ······127	laid with tolerance ······179
heighten ······121	incorporate ······143, 169	landing······55
helpful ······165	increase······121, 123	landscape······19
hesitate ······155	increase~times more ······123	landscape format ······143
hidden ······39	increase work efficiency ······39	latest ······31, 147
hide the ends ······179	indirect light ······79	layout ······86, 87
high in quality······29	initial ······151	leave A to B ······159
high-grade ······25	insect ······21	leeway ······161
high-resolution ······143	insect-proof······21	left over from ······147
high-rise building ······129	insert ······27, 121, 141	legacy ······123
highlight ······71, 121	insist ······85	let~know ······137
hipped roof ······101	insist on ······85	let me ······115
hold ······99, 147	inspection ······129, 167, 181	let's ······49
hopper windows ······65	install ······17, 23, 51, 179	level ······167
horizontal ······51	installation ······77	lift from ······71
horizontal and vertical ······175	installed between ······111	lift the spirits ······25
horizontal louver ······51	instructions ······175	lifted ······71
hotel reception ······47	insufficient ······29	light bulb ······129
housing complex ······36	insulation ······106, 111	lighter ······55
how about~? ······97, 131	intense ······165	lighting ······78
how detailed should we~? ······159	interest ······85	lights in a recess ······71
how to make a request ······152	interfere ······45	limited ······39, 67
humid ······101	interior ······27, 82, 84, 90	limited budget ······49, 67
hustle and bustle ······75	internal ······27, 45, 75	linoleum flooring ······91
	intersection······23	lived-in feel······29
■ I	introduce ······115, 165	lively ······87
I'm afraid that ······139	introduce A to B ······147	living room ······57
ideas like ······41	introduction ······43	load ······51, 63, 137
identify ······119	investigate ······97	locate ······11
if necessary ······135	investigation ······133	locate A in the center of B ······11
if you wish to ······117	invoice ······155	location ······10, 27
illegible ······145	involved in ······157	look after ······115
	issue of ······123	look for ······183

look forward to ······181	might be ······119	omit ······99
look toward(s) ······61	mimic ······85	on both sides ······31
loose ······171	minimum amount ······39	on site······49, 147, 153, 173
lose interest ······85	mirror polished ······17	on the opposite side of the road
loss ······133	mock-up ······177	······79
louver door ······107	model······169	on the safe side ······161
louver windows ······65	modest ······73	on time ······161
louvers ······51	modification ······165	once······73
low budget ······165	modified into ······45	one-side corridor type ······37
low-cost architecture ······48	modify ······45	online server ······143, 151
lower ······97	moire effect······81	opacity ······81
luxurious······19, 73, 91	mold ······55	opaque······81
	monthly ······129	open ······68
■ M	monthly inspection ······129	opening ······62
machinery ······175	more than anticipated ······171	open inwards ······65
machinery room ······105	mortar bedding······111	open space ratio ······95
main bedroom······57	mortar screed ······111	open to ······69
main entrance ······17, 25	motivation······147	opening ······69, 107
main road ······13	motor van ······45	opportunity ······115, 153
maintain ······25	mount~on board ······143	opposite ······79
maintain privacy······25	move onto the next ······115	oppressive ······27, 67
maintenance ······21, 65, 89	movement joint ······111	oppressiveness ······29
maintenance cost ······127	movement of the sun······61	option ······115, 117, 131
maintenance space ······103		order ······145, 163
make a difference ······37	■ N	orientation······151
make a plan compact ······121	namely ······167	original ······143
make a presentation······153	narrow~down ······117	out of date······137
make adjustments ······171	narrowness ······15	oval ······31
make arrangements ······159	natural air-flow system ······51	overbooking ······131
make~barrier-free ······41	natural environment ······12	owner ······61
make for ······35, 123	natural hot spring ······35	
make inspection easy ······129	nature ······13, 73	■ P
make payment into ······155	necessary ······135	painted wall······91
make reference to ······85	negative pressure······107	paired glass······65
make sure ······49	neighbor ······31	paired glass window ······65
make sure to······173	neighboring community······69	pale ······75
make up for ······163	neither interior nor exterior ······27	panoramic ······61
make use of the landscape (of) ······19	newel ······55	parallel louvers······107
manage ······161, 181	nighttime use ······79	parameter lines ······11
manager ······109, 157	no longer valid ······169	paraphrasing ······120
management ······162	nonetheless······61	park ······22
manner ······83	normally ······97	parquet ······111, 179
mansion ······37	nosing ······55	part of ······19
masonry structure ······101	noted ······141	partition ······69, 71
massiveness ······77	not much A than B······67	pass by ······47
match ······75, 83	not only A but also B······41, 133	passageway ······23, 31
match the regulations ······177	not unified ······15	paste ······145
material ······25, 29, 49, 55, 89	now that ······169	paste on ······145
mature city ······119		path ······59
maximum height limit ······37	■ O	pattern······81
mechanical service room ······129	obstruction ······61	paved with ······19
mesh glazing ······65	occupy ······39, 47	pavement ······23
method ······101, 129	offer ······117	payment ······154, 155
microcosmos ······27	office ······38	penalty charge ······157

pendant ⋯79	private house ⋯34	recognize beauty in ⋯33
pendant lighting ⋯79	private space ⋯53	recommend ⋯87, 117
perforated ⋯81	private view ⋯147	reconfirm ⋯175
perforated panel ⋯111	proceed ⋯157	reconsider ⋯161
permitted ⋯37	profitable ⋯139	rectangular ⋯11, 31
personal ⋯39	profitability ⋯127	red lined ⋯163
personal belongings ⋯39	procedure ⋯153	redevelopment ⋯15, 147
personnel ⋯163	project ⋯145, 157	reduce echo ⋯111
perspective ⋯43, 99	project brief ⋯141	reduce the cost ⋯49, 121, 131
philosophy ⋯139	project experience ⋯141	reduce the load of ⋯51
photo shoot ⋯182, 183	projection screen ⋯39	reduction ⋯53, 165
photographer ⋯183	promenade ⋯11	refer to ⋯135
piling ⋯175	promote ⋯87	reference ⋯43, 85
pivot windows ⋯65	proposal ⋯131	reference corner ⋯33
plan ⋯57	propose ⋯116	reflect ⋯75
planning ⋯56	propose options ⋯130	reflect light ⋯75
planning permission ⋯97	proposed for ⋯35	reflected lighting ceiling plan ⋯79
planting ⋯17, 20	proposing ideas ⋯116	reflection ⋯11, 79, 183
planting plan ⋯21	proposing options ⋯130	refreshing impression ⋯33
plaster ⋯91, 177	pros and cons ⋯133	refurbish ⋯49, 53
please find ⋯155, 171	prosperous ⋯13	refurbished with ⋯99
plenty ⋯33	provide ⋯45, 81	refurbishment ⋯52
plenty of natural light ⋯33	provide a sense of ⋯17	regular ⋯167
plinth ⋯103	pub ⋯45	regular site inspection ⋯167
polygon ⋯31	public building ⋯40	regulation ⋯177
poor ⋯73	public meeting ⋯95	reinforced concrete ⋯101
positioned ⋯109	public open space ⋯23, 95	reinforced concrete structure ⋯101
positioning of ⋯61	public space ⋯42	reject ⋯131
possible ⋯79	public square ⋯43	relation ⋯91, 157
postbox ⋯109	pursue ⋯49	relevant ⋯141
potential ⋯47, 123		reliable ⋯165
potential customers ⋯47, 117	■ Q	religious ⋯83
PPE kit ⋯167	quake-absorbing structure ⋯99	religious manner ⋯83
PPT slide ⋯145	qualified ⋯141	renovate ⋯53, 127
prayer ⋯75	qualified architect ⋯141	renovation ⋯52, 133
pre-stressed concrete ⋯99	quality ⋯29	rentable floor area ratio ⋯127
prefabrication ⋯49	query ⋯135, 155	rental income ⋯127
prefabricated method ⋯101	quick drink after work ⋯45	rental cycle ⋯43
preliminary design ⋯168, 169	quotation ⋯170, 171	repeated use ⋯77
prepare ⋯57, 131		replace ⋯129
presence ⋯67	■ R	require ⋯39, 45, 79, 95, 169
presentation ⋯19, 115	rainy conditions ⋯91	require time and money ⋯53
preserve ⋯89, 123	raised access floor ⋯123	requirement ⋯125
prevent ⋯55, 81, 111	raised floor ⋯103	resident ⋯63, 87, 95
prevent A from B ⋯25	ramp ⋯97	resource ⋯123
prevent~ing ⋯81	randomly ⋯27	rest ⋯93
prevent mold ⋯55	randomly laid ⋯27	rest space ⋯43
previous ⋯117, 131, 155	rather than ⋯33, 131	restricted ⋯43
previous firm ⋯141	ratio ⋯39, 95, 127	restriction ⋯95
previously ⋯73	reason ⋯109, 117, 118, 119	retailer ⋯45
print on both sides of the paper ⋯135	reason why ⋯51	reveal ⋯123
	reception ⋯47, 73	revised ⋯121
priority ⋯35, 49	recess ⋯71	revision ⋯151
privacy ⋯15, 25, 63	recognize ⋯59	revision note ⋯151

ridge	101	
right	173	
right cost	173	
right procedure	153	
riser	55	
roadway	23	
robust	77	
rocket	73	
road	11, 95	
role	158	
roof eaves	17	
roof tile	89	
rooftop garden	19	
room	161	
room for reconsideration	161	
rough	77	
rough finish	89	
roughly	51	
rounded off	87	
route	59	
runner	91	
running costs	123	
rural area	35	
■ S		
sacrifice	49	
sacrifice the comfort of living	49	
safe	161	
same as	145	
sample	118	
sandblast	91	
sash	65	
save onto an online server	151	
saving energy	51	
say	135	
scale	66	
scarcement	19	
scenery	133	
schedule	67, 160, 161	
schedule management	162	
scheme	157	
scratch-proof	89	
sealing joint	179	
search for	183	
section	99	
security	108, 109	
see A through B	61	
send as an attachment	151	
senior resident	87	
sense	21, 57, 69, 71	
sense of being one space	71	
sensor-controlled	79	
separate	59	
sequence	58	

series of	19	
serve	47	
service(s)	102, 103	
service entrance	17	
service parking space	17	
service room	129	
set back~from	11	
several	29, 125	
severe	65	
shading	74	
shadow restriction	95	
shakeproof	101	
shape	31	
shape of	119	
shared folder	167	
shared house	37	
shared space	53	
shed roof	101	
sheet of paper	135	
shell structure	101	
shielding	51, 65	
shielding effect against	51	
shiny	77	
shoot	183	
shorten	59, 121	
shorten the period	121	
shortened to	97	
should be	43, 129	
showcase	59	
showy	45	
shutter	65	
side jamb	177	
siding	89	
sign	59	
sign plan	41	
silver birch	35	
similar	119	
simple	35	
simply said	177	
simultaneously	125	
since	117	
single hung windows	65	
site	10, 27	
site boundary	11, 23	
site engineer	175	
site manager	157	
site parameter	119	
site survey	139, 166	
situate	55	
situate on	55	
situated near	35	
situation	32, 57	
size	66	
skirting	89, 177	

skylight	61, 65	
slab	99	
slab soffit	91	
slate	89	
slide	137	
slide adjustment	91	
sliding door	31	
sliding windows	65	
slightly	39, 81, 121	
slightly different from	121	
slip resistance	89, 91	
slip-resistant	25	
slope	67, 97	
sloping ground	13	
smoked glass	45	
smooth	77	
smooth finish	89	
so that	35, 109	
soft water	91	
solar energy generation panel	51	
solar panel	19	
solid	77	
solid wood flooring	91	
solution	13	
soon	139	
sound insulation	111	
sound reflection	111	
south facing room	37	
space for a tripod	183	
spacious	11	
spaciousness	27, 37, 71	
specific	173	
specification	53	
spectators	25	
spiral	57	
spot garden	19	
sprayed material	89	
square	22, 23, 43	
stacking	87	
stacking chairs	87	
stadium	25	
stair riser	55	
stair tread and riser	177	
stand against the wall	143	
stand out	71	
stand out against	83	
standard	85	
starting a presentation	114	
start with	13, 147	
station front	47	
steel-framed reinforced concrete structure	101	
steel-framed structure	101	
steel pipe	101	

steep ·······67	texture·······76	turn into ·······23
step ·······67	than expected ·······67	two-generation family ·······53, 57
stone tile ·······179	thanks to such a wonderful team ··· 181	two-hour fire separation walls 105
storage ·······57		two-storey height volume ·······27
storey ·······27	that is all(that's all) ·······135, 139	typical scene ·······13
street ·······15	that's why ·······13	
street corner ·······93	the blind ·······87	■ U
stretch ·······35	the most effective way to ·······43	uncomfortable ·······133
stretchy ·······77	the most important thing about 127	under the ground ·······103
stringer ·······55	theater complex ·······47	under the rail tracks ·······43
strong wind ·······23	thick ·······73	underway ·······163
structure ·······98, 101, 107	thicken ·······99	unexpected ·······161
structure reinforcement ·······163	thickness ·······67	unified ·······15
subcontractor ·······159	think about ·······63	unit-kitchen ·······67
submission ·······143	thoroughly ·······73	universal design ·······55
submit ·······79	thoroughly covered with ·······73	untouched nature ·······73
suburban district ·······35	three times ·······123	update ·······123
success ·······181	threshold ·······177	updated ·······173
such as ·······125	tidy ·······175	upgrade ·······123
suit ·······83	tied to ·······101	upgraded ·······43
suitable ·······29, 79, 83	tight ·······27, 161	upload to ·······141
suitable for ·······47, 79	tile ·······89, 111	uploaded to ·······141
sun-shielding sheet ·······65	tile sample ·······153	upper ·······65
sunshine received ·······37	tilted ·······29	up-to-date drawings ·······153
supervise ·······147	timber ·······101	urban planning ·······43
surface ·······81	timber bearer ·······111	use for ·······85
surrounded ·······73	timber building ·······105	use the maximum floor-area ratio ·······27
surrounded by ·······13, 35, 73	timber structure ·······101	
surroundings ·······167, 177	timber structure house ·······107	use~as a reference ·······43
surrounding buildings ·······15	tiny site ·······27	used as ·······129
surrounding conditions ·······143	to be honest ·······85	used to ·······47
surrounding scenery ·······133	to fit with the surroundings ···177	utilize ·······41
suspended ceiling ·······91	to prevent crime ·······65	
sustainability ·······51	together with ·······119, 129	■ V
sustainable architecture ·······50	toilet ·······57	vacation villa ·······35
swing windows ·······65	toilet cubicle ·······31	vague ·······171
switch box ·······103	tolerance ·······179	various ·······57
	topic ·······115	vehicle ·······43
■ T	totally ·······23, 145	ventilation ·······51, 55, 65, 106
take a photo ·······183	totally different ·······145	ventilation tower ·······103
take~back and check ·······137	tough ·······77	verge ·······101
take care of ·······161	tough enough ·······77	version ·······131, 137
take into consideration ·······23	toward(s) ·······61	very tight ·······161
take more time ·······163	townscape ·······14, 15, 133	via ·······11, 25
take time to ·······97	traditional construction method 101	view ·······13, 60
take-out ·······45	tranquil ·······75	view of ·······61
tape measure ·······167	transform into ·······15	villa ·······35
target ·······127	translucent ·······81	vinyl sheet (tile) flooring ·······91
target for ·······127	transparency ·······80, 81	visitors ·······33
tatami mat ·······91	trapped ·······179	visitors parking space ·······17
telephone ·······155	tread ·······55	visual ·······69
tension ·······99	trend ·······85	volume ·······26, 95
terrace ·······17, 57	triangular ·······31	
terrazzo ·······91	tripod ·······183	

■ W

wall	179
wall greening	129
wall paper	91
wall shadow gap	179
wall structure	101
warm climate	111
water tank	103
waved	31
way direction	31
way it looks	145
welcome	27, 71, 111
well coordinated	61
wet area	55
what is~like?	109
what kind of?	157, 183
what would be the best time for~?	183
wheelchair user	31
whether to install A or B	19
which is better?	77
while	17, 69
whilst	29, 75
who will pay~?	155
whole	61
whole family	35
why don't we?	117
wide	69
width	95
wild nature	13
window	64, 65
window frame	177
with an actual 1:1 scale mock-up	177
with both hands	175
with depth	67
with the expectation that	81
with the motivation to	147
with these reasons	119
with tolerance	179
within expectations	171
within the last~years	141
without reflections in the glass	183
wonderful	181
wooden	71
wooden house	105
wooden(timber) structure	101
work efficiency	39
work on	83
work together with	181
would be	79
would be the best option	115
would it be possible to~?	153
would like to talk about	177
would love to	21

■ Others

1/500 scale model	169
24-hour fan	107

日本語索引

■あ
間（〜の） …………………63
間にクリアランスをつくる …179
間に設置される ……………111
曖昧な ………………27, 71, 171
曖昧な仕切り ………………71
曖昧な場所……………………27
相見積もり …………………171
相見積もりを取る …………171
合う …………………………83
赤線で描かれた ……………163
明るい色の …………………55
明るさ ………………………78
空き家…………………………53
飽きる ………………………85
アクセス可能な ……………129
アクティビティ ……………92
上げ下げ窓……………………65
上げ床 ………………103, 123
アジア風………………………21
遊びをとって ………………179
暖かみを与える ……………71
厚い …………………………73
厚さ …………………………67
圧縮 …………………………99
圧迫感がある ………………27, 67
圧迫感を避ける ……………29
アップロードされた ………141
アップロードする …………141
集まる ………………………63
集まる場所……………………41
アトリウム……………………23
アプローチ……………………24
甘い …………………………171
雨戸 …………………………65
雨樋 …………………………101
網目ガラス……………………65
粗い …………………………77
粗い仕上げ……………………89
合わせる………………………29

■い
言い換える …………………120
言い換えると ………………121
良い点と悪い点 ……………133
以下の概略のとおり ………117
生け垣 ………………………17
居心地のよくない …………133
維持管理………………………21
維持管理のために …………89
維持する………………………89
石タイル………………………179

維持費 …………………123, 127
衣装室…………………………57
以上です ……………………139
以前の（に）……73, 117, 131, 141
一押しの案 …………………131
位置する………………………47
一点鎖線 ……………………11
一度 …………………………73
一度〜すれば ………………73
一部として……………………19
一面覆われる ………………73
一連の ………………………19
一緒に ………………………129
一緒に働く …………………181
一方で ……………17, 29, 69, 75
いつまでに …………………177
いつも ………………………175
田舎の地域……………………35
イニシャル …………………151
犬走り ………………………19
祈り …………………………75
居間 …………………………57
違約金 ………………………157
〜以来 ………………………117
色 …………………………74, 75
インスタレーション ………77
インテリア ………………82, 84

■う
上枠 …………………………177
浮き上がった ………………71
浮き彫りにする ……………123
浮床下地 ……………………111
受け壁…………………………25
受付 ………………………47, 73
受け渡し ……………………150
薄い（色彩的に）……………75
内側の…………………………45
内倒し窓………………………65
内に開く………………………65
打ち放しコンクリート …89, 101
美しさを見出す ……………33
雨天時の………………………91
促す …………………………87
生まれ変わる ………………15
嬉しい …………………147, 181

■え
映画館併設の…………………47
駅前 …………………………47
閲覧コーナー ………………33
得る ………………………27, 63

円形の ………………………31
演出する …………………33, 81
エントランス…………………24

■お
応じて ………………………53
横断歩道………………………23
応募案 ………………………143
応募する ……………………141
応募要項 ……………………135
覆う …………………………17
オートロック ……………25, 109
オーナー………………………61
オーバーブッキング ………131
大まかな ……………………161
覆われた …………………73, 81
おかげで（〜の）……………181
お客 …………………………181
置く ………………………39, 55
屋上庭園 ……………………19
奥まった場所…………………71
奥行き…………………………67
遅らせる ……………………161
行う …………………………175
納まりの施工 ………………176
納まりの表現 ………………178
収まる ………………………125
納まる ………………………11
教える ………………………137
お勧めする……………………87
落ち着いた …………………75
落ち着かない ………………133
音の反響 ……………………111
踊り場…………………………55
同じ量の ……………………133
お願いの仕方 ………………152
オフィス………………………38
オプションを提示する ……130
お店 …………………………45
おめでとう …………………181
思い浮かぶ …………………125
親柱 …………………………55
折り上げ照明 ………………71
音楽堂 ……………………47, 111
音響 …………………………111
温暖な気候 …………………111
オンラインサーバー ……143, 151

■か
海岸 …………………………13
開口 …………………………107
開口部 ……………………62, 69

外構	16
開催する	147
介して	11
会社	121
改修	133
改修する	49, 53, 99, 127
改善される	43
改善する	43
外装材	91
外装材とする	81
改装された	45
外装	107
解体する	161
階段	67
改訂	151
改訂履歴	151
回転窓	65
外部の	27
外壁	69
解法	13
概要	115, 143
概要を説明する	115
回覧する	137, 173
変える	41
帰る	137
関わらず(〜にも)	61
限られた	39, 67
限られた予算	49, 67
描く	75
家具製作者	159
確認する	49, 141, 157
家具の配置	86, 87
額縁	177
隔離された	75
隔離する	75
隠れた	39, 177
崖	69
囲まれた	35, 73
囲われている	105
風通し	37
画像処理	182
家族全員	35
形	119
形づけられる	31
片流れ屋根	101
塊の	77
傾いた	29
片廊下型	37
花だん	17
勝ち負けが生じる	179
かつては〜していた	47
活発な	87
角	29
必ず〜するようにする	173

可能である	79, 141
可能な限り	73
カビ	55
壁構造	101
壁底目	179
壁に沿って	57
壁に立てかかる	143
〜かもしれない	119
ガラスに映り込まないで	183
ガラリ戸	107
ガルバリウム鋼板	89
枯山水庭園	19
側桁	55
為替レート	171
瓦	89
代わりに	151
代わりの	117
考え	27
考える	63
感覚	57
換気	51, 55, 65, 106
換気塔	103
観客	25
環境	13
環境に優しい	51
関係者用駐車場	17
歓迎する	27
関して	157
感じる	69
緩衝帯	27
頑丈な	77
感じを与える	17
感じを出す	21
関する(〜に)	91
完成	169
完成後に	127
完成する	157, 181
間接照明	79
幹線道路	13
完全に	73
簡単に言うと	177
観点から	43, 99
看板	31
管理エリア	59
管理スペース	103
管理する	161, 181
関連した	141

■き

機会	115
機械	175
機械室	105
機械設備室	129
機会を与える	153

機会を得る	153
気軽に立ち寄れるように	47
期間を短縮する	121
期限切れ	137
記載されている	141
基準に	17
傷つける	179
傷のつきにくい	89
犠牲にする	49
既存建物	49
既存の	67
期待	81
議題	115, 139
期待して	81
期待する	123
きっと〜だろう	115
木の	101
厳しい天候向き	65
木ブロック床材	179
気分を高める	25
基本設計	168, 169
気前よく使うこと	21
決められる	95
決める	163
逆に	49
客間	57
吸音材	111
休憩所	43
休憩する	93
吸収する	75
急上昇する	73
急な	67
境界	57
競技場	25
強調する	71, 121
協働者	97
協働する	141
共同の	73
強風	23
業務	41
鏡面仕上げの	17
共有フォルダー	167
共有部分	53
共用空間	25
許可された	37
許可する	167
漁業	13
極端な	79
拒否する	131
許容誤差	179
切妻屋根	101
議論	93
議論から生まれる	93
際立つ	83

銀行口座 ……………………155	現在 ………………………169	広大さ …………………27, 71
近隣住民……………………31	現在進行中の ………………163	後退した ……………………11
近隣のコミュニティー………69	現在の …………………125, 163	後庭 …………………………57
	現時点で ……………………125	勾配 …………………………97
■く	現時点での変更 ……………133	勾配規制 ……………………97
杭 …………………………175	原寸 …………………………177	高品質建材 …………………25
空間の一体感………………71	喧騒 ……………………15, 75	高品質な ……………………29
空間表現 ……66, 68, 70, 72	現存する ……………………67	構法 …………………100, 101
空気環境 …………………107	現代の生活 …………………83	効率 …………………………49
空地率 ………………………95	建築環境 …………………110	考慮して設計する …………111
空調 ……………………23, 63	建築基準法 …………………23	考慮する …………51, 55, 63
区切り ………………………69	建築許可 ……………………97	高齢者の住人 ………………87
躯体むき出しの内装 ………45	建築物 ………………………23	高齢の ………………………93
クッション床 ………………91	減築 …………………………53	超える ……………………165
杏摺り ……………………177	現地調査 …………139, 166	コーキング材 ……………179
組み合わせることで ……105	現地で ……………………119	ご確認ください …………155
組み立て ……………………49	検討 ………………………133	心地よい ……………………33
組み立て式 …………………49	検討したうえでの提案 ……133	個室トイレ …………………31
曇りガラス …………………45	検討する ……53, 97, 119, 125	個人住宅 ……………………34
暗い ………………………139	現場監督 …………………157	個人の ………………………39
比べる ……………………120	現場検査 …………………167	個人の所有物 ………………39
クリアラッカー仕上げの…91	現場周辺の情報 …………167	コストがかかる ……………49
繰り返しの使用……………77	現場で ……………………153	コスト管理 ………………164
グリッド番号 ……………151	現場で確認する …………173	コストの説明をする ……126
車 ……………………………43	現場での組み立て …………49	コストを削減する …49, 121, 131
車いす専用駐車場 …………17	現場のエンジニア ………175	こだわる ……………………85
車いす利用者 ………………31	建蔽率 ………………………95	子ども部屋 …………………57
クロス（壁紙）……………91		この段階で ………………169
加える ……………………171	■こ	この程度の ………………171
	厚意で ……………………147	このような理由で ………119
■け	公園 …………………………22	コミュニティセンター……17
蹴上 …………………55, 177	効果 ……………………25, 51	木漏れ日 ……………………21
計画 ………………………157	公開空地 ………………23, 95	コルク床 ……………………91
計画された …………………47	高解像度 …………………143	これで終わりです ………135
計画に関わる ……………157	郊外の地域 …………………35	根拠に ……………………119
蛍光灯 ………………………79	高架下 ………………………43	根拠を示す ………………118
傾斜地 ………………………13	効果がある …………………43	コンクリート基礎 ………111
形状 …………………………30	交換する …………………129	コンクリートスラブ ……111
継続して ……………………87	工期 …………………………67	混雑 …………………………33
契約 …………………156, 157	高級感のある ………………73	混雑した ……………………59
契約を締結する …………157	高級感を出す ………………91	コンセプトを検討する ……119
経路 …………………………59	公共空間 ……………………42	混沌 …………………………33
景色 …………………………61	公共建築 ……………………40	困難だ ………………………15
景色を遮る …………………17	公共施設 …………………127	コンパクトにする ………121
結論 ………………………139	公共の広場 …………………43	コンペティション ………141
結論付ける ………115, 157	広告 …………………………45	
結論として ………………139	交差点 ………………………29	■さ
原案 ………………………143	格子状の線 …………………29	再開発 ……………………15, 147
減額を調整する …………165	工場 ………………………153	再確認 ……………………175
玄関 …………………………57	更新する …………………123	最近～年以内で …………141
言及する …………………135	硬水 …………………………91	再考する …………………161
現行案 ……………………127	構造 …………………………98	再考の余地 ………………161
検査 ………………129, 181	高層ビル …………………129	最後に ……………………165
建材 ……………………29, 55	構造補強 …………………163	最後の ……………………145

最小限の量	39	
最初に	49	
最新の	31, 147	
最新版の	137, 153, 173	
最善（ベスト）を尽くす	165	
再チェック	177	
サイディング	89	
最適の時間はいつですか？	183	
彩度	74	
最優先	35	
採用する	51, 157	
在来工法	101	
最良の	115	
サイン計画	41	
差が生まれる	37	
栄えた	13	
探す	183	
酒場	45	
桜	21	
避ける	61, 179	
支える	99	
サステイナブル	50	
〜させてください	115	
撮影	182	
サッシ	65	
雑用	163	
様々な	29, 57, 125	
様々な観点から	125	
様々な状況で	57	
妨げる	45, 81	
さらなる	175	
さらに	41	
さわやかな印象	33	
三角形	31	
参加する	141	
三脚	183	
三脚用のスペース	183	
参照	43	
参照する	43, 85	
残念ですが	139	

■し

仕上げ	19, 88, 90	
仕上げ材	49	
仕上げの段階で	163	
シークエンス	58	
シェアハウス	37	
シェル構造	101	
死角	109	
視覚上の	69	
視覚上のつながりのために	69	
資格のある	141	
資格のある建築士	141	
四角形	31	

時間がより掛かる	163	
〜時間耐火壁	105	
時間と費用がかかる	53	
敷地	10	
敷地境界線	11, 23	
敷地境界	119	
敷モルタル	111	
事業計画	127	
資源	123	
仕事上がりの"軽い"一杯	45	
持参する	131	
指示	175	
指針	127	
自然換気	51	
持続可能性	51	
〜したい	177	
時代	41	
下請け	159	
従って	95, 97	
下に	103	
下に位置する	17	
下町地域	147	
〜したらどうだろうか？	117	
しっかりした	77	
漆喰	91	
湿気のある	101	
しっくい	177	
実現可能な	125	
実施設計	172	
実務経験	141	
質問	135, 155	
質問をする	134	
質問を受ける	135	
〜していただけますか？	153	
〜していただけると助かります（幸いです）	147, 165	
〜してもよろしいでしょうか？	135	
自転車道	23, 43	
支払い	154, 155	
支払いをする	155	
絞る	117	
染み出す	93	
市民	41	
市民のための	41	
締めくくる	138	
指紋	91	
指紋防止	91	
写真家	183	
写真撮影	183	
写真を撮る	183	
借景として利用する	19	
車道	23	
遮蔽	51	

遮蔽した	65	
邪魔な	75	
砂利	17, 19	
砂利の小路	25	
斜路	67, 97	
周囲に	103	
周囲の景観	133	
収益性	127	
集客性がある	33	
宗教上の	83	
宗教上のマナー	83	
重厚感	77	
集合住宅	36	
重視する	37	
修正する	163	
集中する	93	
集中力を上げる	39	
集中を促す	93	
充填材	179	
住人	95	
十分な	33, 63, 79	
十分に	77, 129	
周辺環境	12, 14	
周辺条件	143	
周辺に合わせて	177	
周辺の建物	15	
周辺を囲まれている	13	
住民	63	
住民説明会	95	
重要項目	37	
重要な	127	
重要な点は〜だ	127	
主玄関	25	
主出入口	17	
主寝室	57	
竣工	180, 181	
順番	145	
準備する	57, 131	
〜しよう	49	
小宇宙	27	
省エネルギー	51	
紹介する	115, 147, 165	
障害物	61	
障がい者専用駐車場	17	
消火器	103	
状況	57, 73	
商業化する	43	
商業施設	19, 44, 46	
商業地域	95	
商業の	95	
詳細情報	137, 141	
詳細図面	159	
正直に言うと	85	
少々お時間をください	137	

使用する……………………85	滑り止めの……………………25	潜在顧客が通る場所……………47
状態………………………32	住み心地を犠牲にする………49	潜在的な……………………47, 123
承認する……………………95, 97	図面……………………121, 143	繊細な仕上げ……………………89
消費行動……………………47	図面一式………………………169	全然違う………………………145
丈夫な………………………85	図面縮尺………………………151	全体……………………………61
上部の………………………65	スライド………………………137	全体的に………………………23
照明…………………………78	スライド調整…………………91	選択肢……………115, 117, 131
照明天井伏図…………………79	スラブ……………………………99	前庭……………………………57
常緑樹…………………………21	スラブ下端……………………91	選定する………………………159
植栽…………………………17, 20	～することは可能ですか?…153	前面道路……………………11, 95
植栽計画………………………21	～するために…………………35	前面道路に接する………………11
職場…………………………141	～するのは難しい…………107, 133	専有部分………………………53
所有物…………………………39	～するべきだ………………43, 129	
書類…………………………137	～するように…………………109	■そ
白樺……………………………35	～するよりも…………………131	増加する……………………121, 123
資料の確認……………………150	スレート………………………89	総合設計制度……………………23, 95
遮蔽効果………………………51		総合的な…………………………23
人員…………………………163	■せ	掃除する………………………123
進行管理………………………162	正確な…………………………173	想像上の水の流れ………………19
進行中の………………………163	正確を期す…………………171, 173	増築………………………………53
人工緑葉………………………129	生活感…………………………29	想定………………………………57
伸縮性…………………………179	請求……………………………154	想定内の………………………171
伸縮性のある……………………77	請求書…………………………155	挿入する…………27, 121, 141
伸縮性を考慮する……………179	制限された……………………43	促進する………………………35
伸縮継手………………………111	成功……………………………181	即答を避ける…………………136
申請書…………………………143	制作過程………………………145	側面……………………………125
人造大理石……………………91	正式な手続き…………………153	素材……………………………29
新築…………………………133	成熟都市………………………119	組積造…………………………101
しんどい………………………161	贅沢な演出……………………19	沿って………………………31, 57
信頼できる……………………165	性能……………………………53	外の………………………………11
	製本……………………………143	備える……………………………45
■す	製本する………………………143	それぞれの段階で……………157
水準器…………………………167	整理する………………………175	それでは～はどうか?…………131
推薦する………………………117	責任として(～の)……………157	それゆえに………………………13
水平垂直………………………175	セキュリティ…………………108	揃えた……………………………67
水平の……………………………51	施工業者…………………153, 159	存在感……………………………67
水平ルーバー………………51, 107	施工現場………………………174	存在感がある……………………67
据える……………………………11	施工入札………………………173	
隙間………………………103, 179	施工費……………………………49	■た
隙間(～の)……………………103	施工方法…………………………49	耐火……………………………104
隙間風…………………………107	施工予定………………………159	耐火壁…………………………105
すぐさま…………………………59	設計・監理を行う……………147	耐火性の………………………105
すぐに終わる…………………139	石こう…………………………177	耐火フォーム…………………103
優れた…………………………119	切削する………………………175	大気汚染………………………43
スケジュールが厳しい………161	絶対に…………………………161	耐久性…………………………165
スケジュールの確認…………160	設置する…………17, 23, 51, 179	対して……………………………51
少し………………………………81	設備……………………………102, 103	対処する…………………………65
少しばかり………………………39	説明……………………………171	耐震性…………………………99
筋交い……………………………99	ぜひ～したい……………………21	耐震性のある……………………49, 53
進める…………………………157	狭い………………………………15	耐震の…………………………101
砂吹き……………………………91	前回の…………………………155	だいたい…………………………51
すなわち………………………167	全景の見える……………………61	台所………………………………57
素晴らしい……………………125, 181	センサー付きの…………………79	耐熱性……………………………49
滑り止め……………………89, 91	潜在的顧客……………………117	対比……………………………85, 121

太陽光発電	19
太陽光発電パネル	51
太陽の動き	61
タイルのサンプル	153
耐える	77
楕円形の	31
多角形の	31
高さ	67, 97
高さ制限	37, 95, 97
高さ制限いっぱいの	37
高さ目一杯まで建てられる	37
～だから	169
ダクト	103
宅配便	151
～だけでなく～も	41
～だけれども	141
多孔質の	81
多孔質パネル	111
多少	121
戦う	109
正しい	173
正しい金額	173
たたずむ	93
畳	91
立ち上がる(機器やソフトが)	137
達成する	181
建具	159
建物外形	31
建物管理人室	109
建てる	17
立てる	105
堅樋	101
堅枠	177
たとえ～でも	53, 165
例えば	125
楽しみにしている	181
ために（～の）	123
ためらう	155
保つ	79
～だろう	79
単純な	35
担当する	83, 115, 161
段取りを決める	159
断熱	106
断熱材	107, 111
段鼻	55
断面	99

■ち

地域	97
小さな敷地	27
チェックしましたか？	151
近い	69
地下階	67

近くに位置する	35
地下に	103
竹林	21
地質調査	175
着色する	75
注意をひく	117
中心に	57
中心に据える	11
中心にする	33
注目	117
注文する	163
駐輪場	17
超過する	95
調査する	97
調整	159
調整された（きちんと）	61
調整する	171, 181
挑戦的な	131
眺望	60
長方形の	11
調和する	13, 75
直射日光	51
直接に	129
貯水槽	103
散りばめられた	33

■つ

追加の	67
追求する	49
通過して	25
通勤者	41, 59
通常は	97
通用口	17
通路	31
使われる	129
突き出し窓	65
次の理由で	117
次へ移る	115
造り付けの棚	87
続く	25
集う	93
つながり	69
つながる（～を経て）	25
つなぐ	63
坪庭	19
積み上げ椅子	87
積み上げ式の	87
ツヤのある	77
吊り具	91
吊り下げられた	79
吊り天井	91

■て

提案書の作成	142

提案する	35, 116, 117
定義する	95
定期的な	167
提供する	45, 81
提出者	151
提出する	79
訂正された	121
程度	125
定番の	85
適している	183
適切な	79, 97, 107, 111
テクスチャー	76
手頃な価格	29, 37
手すり	87, 89, 177
哲学	139
手つかずの自然	73
鉄筋コンクリート	101
鉄筋コンクリート造	101
鉄骨造	101
鉄骨鉄筋コンクリート造	101
鉄パイプ	101
～ではあるが	57, 125
手配する	151
出窓	65
テラス	17, 57
電気室	129
電気配線用管	103
電球	129
典型的な風景	13
点検をしやすくする	129
点在する	39
電子書籍	41
天井	71, 111, 177
天井底目	179
天井パネル	91
天井廻り縁	177
天井面	179
電柱	15, 61
天然温泉	35
添付された	155
添付として送る	151
添付物	151
天窓	61
電話でお話ししたように	155

■と

～とある	135
ドア枠	177
トイレ	57
同意する	63, 163
統一感がない	15
投影スクリーン	39
投影する	145
動機	147

同時に …………43, 63, 125	体に見せる …………179	配電箱 …………103
動線　　～31, 45, 58, 129	波打った …………31	～倍に増える …………123
どうぞお気軽にご連絡ください…155	なめらかな …………77	配慮 …………87
どうですか？（～は）………97	均しモルタル …………111	配慮する …………23, 105
導入 …………43	なる（～に）…………23	激しい …………165
同封した～をご査収ください …171	軟水 …………91	運び込む …………175
同封する …………171		挟まった …………179
透明度 …………80, 81	■に	端 …………177, 179
同様に …………145	似合う …………83	はしご …………175
同僚 …………93	～において …………37	端に …………39
道路高さ制限 …………95	賑わい …………33	始める …………13, 147
道路の反対側 …………79	二世代家族 …………53, 57	バージョン …………131
通りすぎる …………47	偽物の …………85	柱 …………99
特徴 …………31	似た …………119	パターン …………81
特別な …………173	日光遮蔽シート …………65	バックヤード …………123
特別の配慮 …………101	…にとって～することは難しい…59	発生する …………93
特有の …………15	日本特有の法規 …………94	派手な …………45
都市計画 …………43	庭 …………18	花弁 …………21
閉じた …………93	認識する …………59, 119	跳ね上がる …………73
土台 …………103		幅 …………95
途中 …………161	■ぬ	幅木 …………89, 177
どちらが良いですか？………77	塗り壁 …………91	破風 …………101
突出した …………119		省く …………99
どなたが～を支払いますか？…155	■ね	はめ殺し窓 …………65
どのくらい時間がかかりますか？…97	猫足の …………83	梁 …………99
どの程度～かを検証する…53	ネットにアップロードする …141	バリアフリー化する …………41
どのような～ですか？………157	～年間で …………123	梁せい …………99
ドーム構造 …………101		貼る …………145
留められる …………101	■の	バルコニー …………61, 177
ともに …………119	納期 …………163	パワーポイントのスライド …145
ドライエリア …………17	濃厚な …………75	挽回する …………163
トラック …………45	農村 …………13	反射 …………11, 79, 183
とりあい …………179	濃淡 …………74	反射する …………75
取り込む …………143	濃度のある空間 …………75	反対の …………79
取り壊す …………99	軒 …………17	半透明の …………81
取り残された …………147	望むなら …………117	判読しにくい …………145
どれほど詳細に～すべきですか？…159	後ほど …………153	ハンマーで打ち付ける …………91
どんな～ですか？………109, 183	伸びる …………35	
	野縁 …………91, 111	■ひ
■な	～のような …………21	日当たり …………37
内部空間 …………75		控えめな …………73
内部でも外部でもない …………27	■は	比較 …………121
内部の …………27	～倍 …………123	比較して …………33, 121
内覧会 …………147	背景 …………115	日影規制 …………95
中で（～の）…………59	背景を説明する …………115	光を反射する …………75
中庭 …………11, 57	背後で …………13	引き立たせる …………45
中の …………131	排除する …………49	引違い窓 …………65
眺められるよう計画する…13	排水 …………17	引っ張り …………99
流れる角度 …………103	排水管 …………103	引き戸 …………31
流れを作る …………29	排水溝 …………17	引き渡し …………180
斜めカットで目地を最小にし、一	配達員 …………109	低く抑える …………67
	配置 …………10, 61	低くする …………97
	配置された …………55, 109	庇 …………101
		ビジネスの …………53

非常階段	109
必要とする	79, 95
必要な	135
避難	59
避難経路	59, 97
批評する	147
微妙に異なる	121
費用	155
費用がかかる	127
表現する	75
標識	59
費用対効果	45
表面	81
開き窓	65
開けている（〜に対して）	69
昼間の採光を得る	63
広い	11, 69
広さ	37
広場	22, 23

■ふ

ファサード	15, 28
負圧	107
ファミリー向けマンション	37
ブース	69
フェンス	17
負荷	51, 63
負荷を低減する	51
不規則に	27
吹き付け材	89
吹き抜け天井	129
複雑性	33
複雑な	69, 125
含める	131
相応しい	29, 47, 79
不十分な	29
防ぐ	25, 55, 81, 111
付属資料	119
普通の	131
不透明性	81
不透明な	81
太くする	99
踏面	55, 177
プライバシー	63
プライバシーに配慮する	15
プライバシーを保つ	25
ブレース構造	101
プレストレストコンクリート	99
プレゼンテーションする	115, 153
プレゼン用データの作成	144
プレファブ工法	101
フローリング	177
プロジェクト概要	141
ブロック（でつくられたもの）	111

風呂場	55, 57
雰囲気	83
雰囲気を生む	21
分譲アパート	37
分析する	119, 125
ふんだんな自然光	33

■へ

ペアガラス	65
ペアガラス窓	65
併設	41
併設された	47
平面計画	56
壁面	179
壁面緑化	129
別荘	35
部屋の機能	54
変更	165
編集	145
ペンダント（吊り下げ型）ライト	79
ベンチ	23

■ほ

方位	151
防音シート	111
防音床	111
防火	104
防火の	105
法規	96, 177
法規に従って	177
棒グラフ（横線工程表）	173
報告すること	139
報告として	171
防湿シート	177
防湿層	111
防塵カメラ	167
防水紙	111
防虫	21
防犯	59
防犯上の理由により	109
防犯のために	17, 65
方法	129
訪問者	33
ボード貼りにする	143
保全する	123
舗装された	19
ホテルの受付	47
〜ほど…ではない	67
歩道	23
ボリューム	26, 27, 95
ボリューム（〜層分の高さのある）	27
本物の	85

■ま

毎月の	129
毎月の点検	129
前に	15
任せる	159
曲がった	31
巻き尺	167
まず始めに	115
また（〜も）	47
街角	93
街並み	14, 147
町の景観	133
待つ	175
全くもって	145
末端を隠す	179
窓	64, 65
間取り	57
窓枠	177
マナー	83
真似をする	85
まぶしい	79
まるで〜のように	87
丸められた	87
廻縁	179
マンション	37

■み

見え方	145
御影石	17
見切り材	91, 179
見込む	123
短くする	59, 121
水回り	55
見せる	59
溝	29, 103
溝の付いた	89
溝を付ける	89
密集地	11, 105
見積もる	173
見積もり	155, 170, 171
見積もりをオーバーする	171
南向きの部屋	37
見開きページ	143
見る（〜を通して）	61

■む

向いている	61
迎え入れる	111
迎える	71
向かって	61
むき出しの躯体	45
無垢材フローリング	91
虫	21
棟	101

■め
明快な……………………41
明確に………………59, 151
明確にする………………71
明度………………………74
メールで…………………167
メールに添付して………143
目指す……………………51
目地………………………179
目地シール………………179
目線の高さの……………69
目立つ……………………71
目の見えない人…………87
メリット・デメリット……133
メリット・デメリットを説明する
………………………132
免震構造…………………99
面する……………………109
メンテナンスに配慮して…21, 65
面取りした目地…………179
面取りする………………29

■も
モアレ効果………………81
もう一度おっしゃっていただけますか？……………153
もう一つの………………117
盲目の……………………87
木造………………………101
木造建築…………………105
木造住宅……………105, 107
木造の……………………71
もしかして………………161
もし必要ならば…………135
もたらす…………………179
持ち上げる………………71
持ち帰って調べる………137
持ち帰り…………………45
モックアップ……………177
最も効果的な方法………43
最も大切なことは………127
最もふさわしい…………139
基づいて…………………23
求める………………39, 45
物置………………………57
物干場……………………57
もはや有効でない………169
問題………………………123

■や
夜間使用…………………79
役所………………………41
役にたつ…………………47
役割分担の確認…………158

野生の自然………………13
家賃収入を得る…………127
屋根庇……………………17
山のふもとにて…………35

■ゆ
有益な……………………139
優先事項…………………49
郵便箱……………………109
遊歩道………………11, 23
床から天井まで………35, 63
床仕上げ…………………111
床タイル…………………111
ユニットキッチン………67
ユニバーサルデザイン…55
緩やかなつながり………71

■よ
良い遺産となる…………123
容易にする………………129
要求された機能を盛り込む…169
用紙………………………135
容積率…………………27, 95
容積率を最大限に使う…27
幼稚園……………………77
ような（〜の）…………21
要望………………………125
要望に沿う………………125
予期せぬ…………………161
横レイアウトとする……143
予算………………49, 67, 165
予算を超える……………165
寄棟屋根…………………101
予想以上に…………67, 171
予想する…………………173
余地………………………161
予定通りに………………161
余白………………………143
読み解く…………………13
余裕………………………161
余裕をもって……………161
より明るい………………133
〜よりむしろ……………33

■ら
ラーメン構造……………101
らせん……………………57
欄干…………………55, 89
ランダムに配置された…27

■り
利益だけでなく、損失も……133
利益と損失………………133
率…………………………95

立面………………15, 29
リノベーション…………52
リノリウム床……………91
略語リスト………………173
理由………………………51
流行の……………………85
理由で（〜の）………11, 35
理由を示す………………118
量……………………37, 123
利用者用駐車場…………17
利用する…………………41
両手で……………………175
両面に印刷する…………135
両面に……………………31
隣家………………………11
隣接した…………………17

■る
ルーバー…………………51
ルーバー窓………………65

■れ
例を示す…………………118
レガシー…………………123
劣悪な……………………73
劣悪な環境にある………73
レンガ造…………………83
レンタブル比……………127
レンタル自転車…………43
連絡を取る………………155

■ろ
廊下………………31, 57, 71
ローコスト………………48
陸屋根……………………101

■わ
分ける………………29, 59
和紙………………………57
わずかな敷地……………27
和風………………………83
和洋折衷の………………83

■英数
ALC パネル………………89
CAD 図面…………………153
FRP 樹脂…………………91
1/500 模型………………169
24 時間換気扇……………107

山嵜一也（やまざき・かずや /Yama）

芝浦工業大学システム理工学部環境システム学科教授、山嵜一也一級建築士事務所代表。1974年東京都生まれ。2000年芝浦工業大学大学院修了。2001年渡英。就職活動（500社以上にコンタクト、断りのレター59通）から英国での建築設計活動を開始。アライズ・アンド・モリソン・アーキテクツ勤務時（2003-2012）には、キングスクロス・セントパンクラス地下鉄駅改修計画（2007-2010）や、ロンドン五輪プロジェクト（招致マスタープラン模型、レガシーマスタープラン、グリニッジ公園馬術競技場の現場監理）を担当。2013年に帰国し、東京に事務所を設立。観光科学博士号を取得（東京都立大学 2022）。女子美術大学非常勤講師（2015-2023）。芝浦工業大学特任教授（2021-2023）。2024年より現職。大学において、グローバル、観光、建築設計を軸に研究・教育活動を展開し、後進の育成に携わる。著書に『イギリス人の、割り切ってシンプルな働き方』(KADOKAWA)。

そのまま使える 建築英語表現

2016年10月 1日　初版第1刷発行
2024年 6月20日　初版第6刷発行

著　者 ………… 山嵜一也
発行者 ………… 井口夏実
発行所 ………… 株式会社 学芸出版社
　　　　　　　　京都市下京区木津屋橋通西洞院東入
　　　　　　　　電話 075-343-0811　〒600-8216

リサーチ協力 ………… 吉田知剛、坂本和子
ネイティブチェック … Jaime Humphreys
装　丁 ………… 藤田康平（Barber）
印　刷 ………… イチダ写真製版
製　本 ………… 新生製本

Ⓒ Kazuya Yamazaki 2016　　　　　　　　Printed in Japan
ISBN978-4-7615-2629-0

JCOPY 〈(社)出版者著作権管理機構委託出版物〉
本書の無断複写（電子化を含む）は著作権法上での例外を除き禁じられています。複写される場合は、そのつど事前に、(社)出版者著作権管理機構（電話 03-5244-5088、FAX 03-5244-5089、e-mail: info@jcopy.or.jp）の許諾を得てください。また本書を代行業者等の第三者に依頼してスキャンやデジタル化することは、たとえ個人や家庭内での利用でも著作権法違反です。

好評既刊書

建築・都市のプロジェクトマネジメント
クリエイティブな企画と運営　　　　　　　　　　　山根 格 著

A5判・200頁・本体2300円+税

多様化・複合化・国際化・横断化が進む建築・都市開発において、既存の社会資本を活かし、社会的な課題にも応えるマネジメントが求められている。都市生活の創造性を高めげる建築・都市をいかにつくるか。チームアップから、品質、デザイン、コスト、スケジュール、リスクのマネジメントまで、わかりやすく解説。

サイト　建築の配置図集
SITES Architectural Workbook of Disposition　　松岡 聡・田村 裕希 著

B5変判・256頁・本体3600円+税

80余りの名作建築を広大な敷地周辺と共に、木の葉や屋根の表情まで微細に再現した図集。敷地周辺図に占める建物図の割合を0.1%から50%へ徐々にズームアップし、地形図から詳細な間取りへと見せ所を変えながら、建物と敷地の関係を多様な広がりで捉え直した。見方のヒントとなる課題を解きながら新たな発想を得るワークブック。

海外で建築を仕事にする
世界はチャンスで満たされている　前田 茂樹 編著、田根 剛ほか 著

四六判・272頁・本体2400円+税

世界と渡り合う17人の建築家・デザイナーのエネルギッシュなエッセイ。A.シザ、H&deM、D.アジャイ他、大建築家達との面談、初の担当プロジェクト、ワーク＆ライフスタイル、リストラ、独立、帰国…、建築という武器と情熱があれば言葉の壁は関係ない。一歩踏み出すことで限りなく拡がる世界を見た実践者から若者へのエール。

海外で建築を仕事にする 2
都市・ランドスケープ編　　　　福岡 孝則 編著、別所 力ほか 著

四六判・272頁・本体2400円+税

建築単体にとどまらず、都市、ランドスケープ、コミュニティデザインまで、パブリックスペースのデザインに挑戦する16人のエッセイ。米国の都市公園で人造湖の設計、バルセロナのバス路線計画、ルーブル美術館来場者のモビリティ分析、メルボルン流まちづくり、アフリカでの実測調査まで、建築のフィールドはまだまだ広い！